It Can't Be Done . . .

What can you conceive more silly and extravagant than to suppose a man racking his brains and studying night and day how to fly?
— *William Law*, A Serious Call to a Devout and Holy Life XI, 1728

Is it not demonstrated that a true flying machine, self-raising, self-sustaining, self-propelling, is physically impossible?
— *Professor Joseph Le Conte*, University of California, 1888

All attempts at artificial aviation are not only dangerous to life but doomed to failure from an engineering standpoint.
— *Editor of* The Times *of London*, 1905

Their Lordships are of the opinion that they would not be of any practical use to the Naval Service.
— *British Admiralty*, in reply to the Wright's offer of patents for their airplane, 1907

In the opinion of competent experts, it is idle to look for a commercial future for the flying machine. There is, and always will be, a limit to its carrying capacity. . . .Some will argue that because a machine will carry two people, another may be constructed that will carry a dozen, but those who make this contention do not understand the theory.
— *W.J. Jackman and Thomas Russell*, Flying Machines; Construction and Operation, 1910

We do not consider that aeroplanes will be of any possible use for war purposes.
— *The British Secretary of State for War*, 1910

There is no hope for the fanciful idea of reaching the moon because of insurmountable barriers to escaping the earth's gravity.
— *Dr. F.R. Moulton*, University of Chicago Astronomer, 1932

The example of the bird does not prove that man can fly. . .
— *Simon Newcomb*, Professor of Mathmatics, Astronomer, U.S. Navy, 1903

MUSEUM OF FLIGHT

100 Years of Aviation History

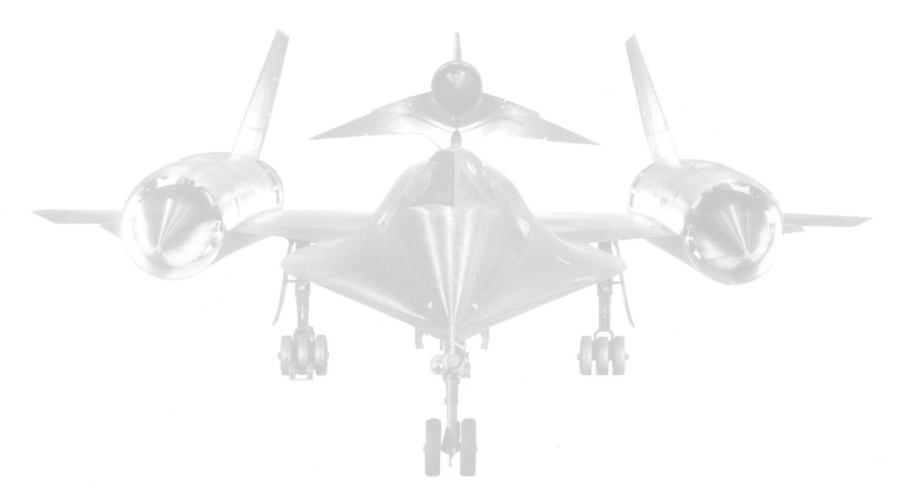

In Association with Stonebridge

MUSEUM OF FLIGHT

100 Years of Aviation History

Seattle Washington

ELTON-WOLF PUBLISHING

Cover design by Beth Farrell
Text design and layout by Beth Farrell, Sheila Hackler, and Paulette Eickman

Text and pictures provided by
Museum of Flight
The Boeing Company
McDonnell Douglas Aircraft Company

Published by Elton-Wolf Publishing
Seattle, Washington

ISBN: 1-58619-039-3
Library of Congress Catalog Number: 2002110363

06 05 04 03 02   1 2 3 4 5

First Edition October 2002

Printed in China

ELTON-WOLF PUBLISHING

Seattle.Washington.98121   www.elton-wolf.com   206.748.0345

This book is dedicated to the brave and forward-thinking men and women
who have made flight their lives and, in so doing,
changed ours.

A Soaring Collection

From the Wright brothers' sand dunes to the surface of the moon, aviation technology grew exponentially in the twentieth century. Although figuring out a way to fly took hundreds of years, once discovered, humankind devised better and better means of air transport at an astounding pace. The Wrights quickly improved upon their first success—by 1905 they had developed a fully practical airplane, the *Flyer* 3. This was followed by rapid design advances on both sides of the Atlantic, and by the time Bleriot crossed the English Channel in 1909, it was clear that these flying contraptions might be useful for more than quick thrills.

Although the Europeans initially lagged in aviation development, they caught up rapidly once military advantages were seen. The fact that planes could be used in warfare presented a whole new host of possibilities. With military funding, aircraft evolution speedily advanced. From World War I–era big planes to the amazing M/D-21 Blackbird spy plane, military use of aircraft has forever changed the way nations interact in times of war and peace. History has changed as a result.

Even as airplanes were altering the face of warfare, they were changing the way people did business on the home front. After the advent of domestic airmail service in 1918, cargo and passenger transport were quickly recognized as potentially lucrative commercial endeavors. Boeing's luxurious Model 80 established a new standard in passenger transport with its comfort and first use of stewardesses. Technical advances in the 1930s and 1940s made flying a more affordable and safer experience, ushering in a golden age for commercial aviation. Then, with the arrival of the jet transport and the groundbreaking impact of aircraft such as Boeing's 747 "jumbo jet," it became clear that airplanes would change the way we view the world.

Having had profound impact on twentieth century history, aircraft are here to stay, and their adaptability to a wide variety of uses has led to new heights of human invention.

Airplane Type	Pre-1910	1910-1920	1920-1930
Civilian			
Commercial			
Experimental			
Military			
Space			
Helicopter			

In Collection

Proposed

Legend

1. Gas Balloon*
2. Curtiss Pusher*
3. Curtiss Robin
4. Cessna CG-2
5. Howard DGA-15
6. Heath Parasol
7. McAllister Yakima Clipper
8. Beech 17 Staggerwing*
9. Stinson SR Reliant
10. Taylorcraft A
11. Aeronca C-2
12. Bowlus BA-100 Baby Albatross
13. Piper J-3 Cub
14. LET LF-107 Lunak
15. ERCO Ercoupe 415-C
16. Stinson 108 Voyager
17. Fairchild 24
18. Lamson Alcor
19. Fournier RF-4D
20. Stephens Akro
21. B & W
22. Boeing B-1*
23. Swallow Commercial
24. Ryan M-1
25. Boeing 40A*
26. Boeing 80A-1
27. Hamilton Metalplane H-47*
28. Alexander Eaglerock
29. Stearman C-3B
30. Boeing 247D
31. Douglas DC-2
32. Douglas DC-3
33. de Havilland D.H.84 Dragon Rapide*
34. Boeing 307B Stratoliner*
35. Lockheed Constellation*
36. Beech C-45H Expeditor
37. Antonov An-2
38. Vickers VC2 Viscount
39. de Havilland D.H. 106 Comet 4C
40. Lockheed Jetstar
41. Boeing 707/VC-137B
42. Boeing 727
43. Boeing 747
44. Boeing 737
45. Concorde*
46. Icarus*
47. de Vinci Ucrella*
48. Lilienthal Glider
49. Bleriot*
50. Chanute-Herring Glider
51. Wright Glider
52. Pitts Special*
53. Bensen B-8M Gyro-Copter
54. Cascade Ultralights Kasperwing
55. Sorrel Parasol
56. Thorp T-18 Tiger
57. Bowers Fly Baby
58. Durand Mk V
59. Aerocar III
60. Rutan Vari Viggen

*Proposed acquisitions

AIRCRAFT COLLECTION

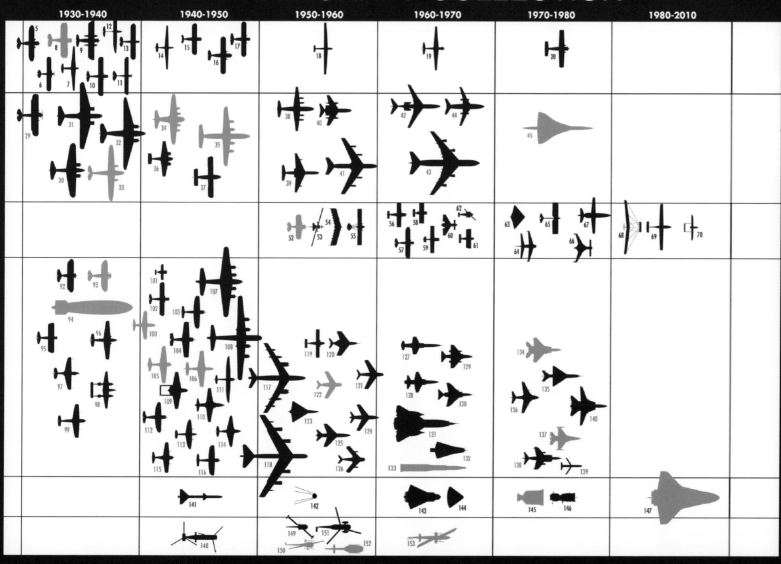

| 1930-1940 | 1940-1950 | 1950-1960 | 1960-1970 | 1970-1980 | 1980-2010 |

WITH THANKS TO:

AIRCRAFT PHOTOGRAPHERS

BB - Brian Baum
DP - Dennis Parks
DF - Dennis Fleischman
EH - Eden Hopkins
GSW - Gordon S. William Collection
HM - Heath Moffatt
JH - Jack Hillard
JM - Jay Miller
MA - Marshall Autry
SK - Steve Keating

CONTRIBUTORS

Richard Bach
Alan Mulally
Buzz Aldrin
Bill Anders
Pinky Nelson

Photos of contributors courtesy of:

Richard Bach - Richard Bach
Alan Mulally - The Boeing Co.
Buzz Aldrin - NASA
Bill Anders - Bill Anders
Pinky Nelson - NASA
The Moon - NASA
Sky images - freeimages.co.uk

Photos and text generously compiled and supplied by:

Bill Hayes
Museum of Flight

Resources for contacts and text:

Marin Faure
Dave Knowlen
Jay Spenser

Wright Bros. to the Moon suggested by:

Michael Friedline
Museum of Flight

And special thanks to sponsors:

Mike Hendrickson
Jeff Huey

61. Aerosport Scamp
62. Rotorway Scorpion
63. Eipper Cumulus VB
64. Rutan Quickie
65. Kolb Ultrastar
66. Rutan Vari-Eze
67. Lear Fan 2100
68. Gossamer Albatross II
69. Task Silhouette
70. Insitu Aerosonde
71. Curtiss JN-4D Jenny
72. de Havilland DH-4*
73. Caproni Ca 20
74. Albatross D. Va

75. Aviatik D.I
76. Fokker Dr.I Triplane
77. Fokker D.VII
78. Fokker D.VIII
79. Fokker E.III
80. Nieuport Type 27
81. Nieuport Type 28
82. Pfalz D.XII
83. Rumpler Taube
84. RAF S.E.5a
85. Sopwith Camel
86. Sopwith Pup
87. Sopwith Snipe
88. Sopwith Triplane

89. SPAD XIII
90. Nieuport Type 24
91. Douglas World Cruiser*
92. Boeing 100/P-12
93. Boeing P-26*
94. Goodyear ZPG-2*
95. Stearman PT-13A Kaydet
96. Nord 1002 (Bf 108)
97. Curtiss P-40N Warhawk
98. Lockheed P-38L Lightning
99. Messerschmitt Bf 109E-3
100. Kawanishi N1K1*
101. Link Trainer
102. Aeronca L-3B

103. Goodyear FG-1D Corsair
104. General Motors FM-2 Wildcat
105. Mitsubishi A6M Zero*
106. North American P-51D Mustang
107. Boeing B-17F Flying Fortress
108. Boeing B-29 Superfortress
109. de Havilland D.H.100 Vampire FB.5
110. Lockheed F-80C Shooting Star
111. Pratt-Read PR-G1
112. Republic P-47D Thunderbolt
113. Supermarine Spitfire Mk.IX

114. Yakovlev Yak-9U
115. Kawanishi NIK2
116. Goodyear F2G-1 Super Corsair
117. Boeing WB-47E Stratojet
118. Boeing B-52G Stratofortress
119. Dornier Do 27
120. Grumman F9F-8 Cougar
121. Canadair CL-13B Sabre
122. Mikoyan-Gurevich MiG-15*
123. Convair XF2Y-1 Seadart
124. Fiat G.91 Pan
125. Vought XF8U-1 Crusader
126. Mikoyan-Gurevich MiG-17
127. Lockheed F-104C Starfighter

128. Northrop YF-5A
129. Douglas A-4F Skyhawk
130. McDonnell F-4C Phantom II
131. Lockheed M-21
132. Lockheed D-21
133. Boeing LGM-30 Minuteman*
134. McDonnell Douglas F-15 Eagle*
135. Mikoyan-Gurevich MiG-21PFM
136. Grumman A-6E Intruder
137. General Dynamics F-16A Fighting Falcon*
138. McDonnell Douglas AV-8C Harrier
139. Boeing AGM-86B ALCM

140. Grumman F-14A Tomcat
141. GAPA
142. Sputnik
143. Mercury Capsule
144. Apollo Command Module
145. Boeing Inertial Upper Stage*
146. Resurs-500
147. Space Shuttle*
148. Piasecki H-21B Workhorse
149. Hiller YH-32 Hornet
150. Hiller UH-12*
151. Sikorsky HH-52 Seaguard
152. Bell UH-1D Iroquois*
153. Bell AH-1 Cobra*

Civilian Aircraft

A bird is an instrument working according to mathematical law, which instrument it is within the capacity of man to reproduce with all its movements.

– *Leonardo Da Vinci*, Treatise on the Flight of Birds, 1505

Richard Bach

He moves not through distance, but through the ranges of satisfaction that come from hauling himself up into the air with complete and utter control; from knowing himself and knowing his airplane so well that he can come somewhere close to touching, in his own special and solitary way, that thing that is called perfection. —Richard Bach, A *Gift of Wings*

There's a replica or two on these pages, to show an outline of how flight began. The rest are real airplanes with real pasts and futures. Real pilots flew them.

I know this, strangely enough, because one of my airplanes, the Pterodactyl Ascender II ultralight, is part of the Museum of Flight collection. It was built from a kit in my garage in Oregon and flown from a hayfield down the road. I measured and drilled and cut and bolted, fastened wires with copper clamps squeezed tight. I covered it all with fabric, set the engine in place, fit the propeller and tightened it on the hub.

I ran the engine for a while and, one day in 1981, I snaked my way into the canvas sling that is the pilot's seat, pushed forward the throttle that I had assembled and attached. The Pterodactyl turned into the wind, skipped once or twice on the grass of the hayfield, swept itself and me along with it into the sky, both our hearts beating fast.

Many the open cockpit I'd flown, none so open as this one. Way in the air, I realized the obvious: there's no floor. Drop my pencil over the forest, it's a 2,000-foot drop, straight down.

What a pleasure, that little kite! Mornings early, before the wind could rise we did, the Pterodactyl and me, over the valley mist melting in cool sunlight. High over the meadows, I reached back and shut the engine off, propeller bumping to a stop, we two became a condor over golden hillsides, gliding. Like other builders professional and amateur, I had given life to an airplane, and by way of thanks it gave life back to me.

So did every other aircraft you see upon these pages give life back to its builders. One particular morning, one certain date not so far back in memory, the Cub, the Fly-Baby, the Fairchild, one day each of these airplanes flew for the first time, took its test pilot aloft.

Behind each photo is a real airplane, behind each airplane is flight itself, expressed in thrust and power, in speed and wind.

We fly, I think, because flying reminds us we're spirit, not flesh. Tie our body to the body of an airplane lifting away from the grass, we remember. Every airplane that's familiar, it's familiar because of our memories, yesterdays or lifetimes gone by. Every one strange to me on these pages is familiar to some other pilot; as I remember the Pterodactyl, they remember a different airframe, a different sunrise, wheels leaving ground and later touching softly back.

These airplanes live. We live. And after our sleeps, we wake and fly again.

—*Richard Bach*, Author and Pilot

Lilienthal Glider

Manufacturer: Lilienthal
Model: 1893 Glider
Year: 1901
Registration: None
Serial No.: Reproduction

Span: 22.96 feet
Length: 16.40 feet
Wing Area: 150.7 square feet
Weight (without pilot): 44 pounds
Weight (with pilot): 220 pounds
Location: Museum of Flight
Viewable

Discovery

The flying knowledge of aerial pioneers like German inventor Otto Lilienthal led directly to the Wright brothers' first flights. Starting in 1891, Lilienthal and his brother built monoplane and biplane gliders with arched, bat-like wings. Lilienthal's first flights, launched from a springboard in his backyard, took him a few meters into the air. After hundreds of test flights, he was able to leap and soar across the entire yard.

The secret to Lilienthal's gliders was cambered or curved wings. He studied birds and their anatomy and developed his gliders' wings with the same arched shape to produce maximum lift. Behind the wings, he built a tail for directional stability. The inventor-pilot squeezed into the fuselage opening and grasped the holding bars. During flight, Lilienthal shifted his weight for control.

Flight

Lilienthal gained experience as a glider pilot on nearby hills, performing flights with remarkable control of his craft. In 1894, he even built an artificial hill so that he could launch his gliders with any wind direction. Otto Lilienthal, the most experienced flyer in the world at the time, was soon searching for higher launch points and stronger winds. Leaps from the Rhinower Hills near Berlin achieved spectacular glides of up to 1,150 feet (345 m).

Sacrifices

Lilienthal thought that flapping wings were the key to powered flight. He even experimented with gliders that had flapping wingtips, powered by a small, carbonic acid gas engine. The inventor never got to fully test his powered machine. On August 9, 1896, he took off from a hill in one of his monoplane gliders when a sudden gust of wind tossed his craft upward. Trying to correct, Lilienthal shifted his weight suddenly forward and the machine took a nosedive into the ground. Otto Lilienthal died the following day. His last words were, "Opfer müssen gebracht werden. (Sacrifices must be made.)"

Chanute-Herring Glider

Manufacturer: Chanute-Herring
Model: 1896 Glider
Year: 1996
Registration: None
Serial No.: Reproduction

Span: 16 feet
Length: 12.3 feet
Height: 7.2 feet
Wing Area: 135 square feet
Weight, without pilot: 23 pounds
Weight, with pilot: 178 pounds
Location: Museum of Flight
Viewable

The Most Successful Pre-Wright Glider

In 1896 Octave Chanute and fellow flying enthusiasts went to wind-swept Miller Beach on Lake Michigan to test three new glider designs. The type seen at the Museum of Flight was actually built as a tri-plane. Early flights revealed to Chanute and co-designer Augustus Herring that the three-winged machine had too much lift, which made it unstable. With the bottom wing removed, it not only outperformed the other designs, but proved at the time to be the most successful glider ever built—with hundreds of controlled flights of up to 359 feet (107 m), for as long as fourteen seconds. Its rigid, truss-supported biplane design became the basis for the Wright brothers' gliders.

Octave Alexander Chanute (1832-1910)

Chanute was born in France and emigrated to the United States at age six. As one of America's leading civil engineers, he designed railroads and bridges before showing an interest in flight. Beyond his experiments with manned gliders, Chanute is important because he collected and studied a wealth of information on flight; from the ancients to the latest aeronautical experimenters of the day. With this knowledge, he encouraged would-be fliers around the world in articles and lectures, and gave many experimenters financial and technical assistance.

The Museum's reproduction glider was built by Boeing engineer and hang-glider pilot Paul Dees for the 100th anniversary of the 1896 flights.

Controlled Flight

Why is this Wright Glider called the most significant aircraft ever built and flown? No, it's not the plane that made history at Kitty Hawk in 1903. However, that aircraft owed its success to the nearly one thousand stability and control flights the Wrights made with this type of glider. The Wrights' experiments with gliders solved the main problem of heavier-than-air manned flight: control.

The original 1902 Wright glider did not survive. It was left at Kitty Hawk and destroyed by the elements.

Axes of Flight

The wires on this glider connect the wing tips to a U-shaped cradle beneath the pilot's hips. When the pilot moves the cradle, he twists the wing tips in opposition to each other, and the glider *rolls* for a turn. Different wires connect the rudder in back to this "wing-warping" mechanism, thus controlling *yaw*. The pilot controls *pitch* by rolling the bar in his hands, which changes the position of the elevator in front.

The Wright Brothers

Orville and Wilbur were always fascinated with machines. Together, they built and sold mechanical toys, published a paper with Orville's own press, and rented and sold bicycles. The brothers became interested in flying after reading of Otto Lilienthal's death in 1896. When their first gliders didn't provide the lift that Lilienthal's calculations said they should, the Wrights built a wind tunnel and compiled the first reliable tables of air pressures on curved surfaces. Their next glider, the 1902 version, had much improved aerodynamic qualities and led the way to their first powered flights the following year.

The Museum's replica glider was built in 1960 by a team of University of Washington Aeronautical Engineering students, supervised by Professor R. G. Joppa.

This aircraft is on loan from the Museum of History and Industry, Seattle, Washington.

Wright Glider

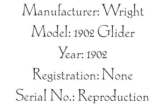

Manufacturer: Wright
Model: 1902 Glider
Year: 1902
Registration: None
Serial No.: Reproduction

Span: 32.08 feet
Length: 16.33 feet
Height: 5.29 feet
Wing Area: 320 square feet
Weight: 116 pounds
Location: Museum of Flight
Viewable

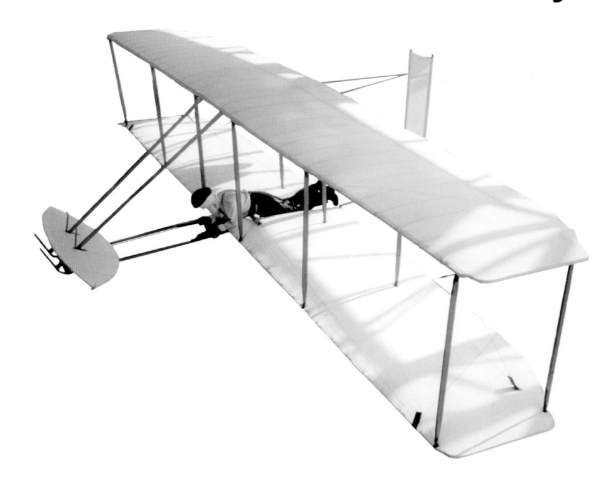

Aeronca C-2

Manufacturer: Aeronca
Model: C-2
Year: 1929
Registration: N30RC
Serial No.: 301-23

Span: 36 feet
Length: 20 feet
Height: 7.5 feet
Wing Area: 142 square feet
Empty Weight: 398 pounds
Gross Weight: 672 pounds
Cruise Speed: 65 mph
Top Speed: 80 mph
Range: 240 miles
Location: Museum of Flight
Viewable

The Flying Bathtub

"Just the basics" was the name of the game with the Aeronca C-2. The pilot sat on a bare plywood seat with five instruments, a stick, and rudder pedals in front of him. If you wanted a heater or brakes—they cost extra. The little plane had odd, almost comical lines that earned it the nickname *The Flying Bathtub*. The C-2 wasn't fast, big, or powerful, but it was one of the first American airplanes to be affordable and economical—characteristics that sold 164 Aeronca C-2s in 1930 and 1931, despite America's financial woes.

Little Engines

Powering the little plane was always a problem. First, Roche installed a borrowed Henderson motorcycle engine but it couldn't get the plane off the ground. Roche turned to Harold Morehouse, who had designed a small engine to pump ballast air into a blimp. It was modified and installed for the Roche Original's first flights. When a crash destroyed that engine, another was fashioned by Roy Poole and Robert Galloway. When the C-2s went into production, they had engines that were cast elsewhere, assembled at Aeronca, and called Aeronca E-107s.

Flight Fact: The C-2 is believed to be the first aircraft to be refueled from a moving automobile. The pilot used a wooden cane to hook a five-gallon can handed from a speeding Austin auto during an air show in California in 1930.

The Museum's 1929 C-2 has an Aeronca E-113 36-hp engine that was used to power heavier Aeronca C-3s.

Curtiss Robin

Manufacturer: Curtiss
Model: C-1 Robin
Year: 1929
Registration: N979K
Serial No.: 628

Span: 41 feet
Length: 25.08 feet
Height: 8 feet
Wing Area: 223 square feet
Empty Weight: 1700 pounds
Gross Weight: 2440 pounds
Cruise Speed: 102 mph
Max Speed: 120 mph
Service Ceiling: 12700 feet
Range: 300 miles
Location: Museum of Flight
Viewable

Not Pretty, But Practical

The Curtiss Robin was designed for private owners. Conventional in many ways, the Robin was popular because it had an unusually large, enclosed cabin and a reasonable price. The dependable Curtiss Robin became one of the most commercially successful airplanes of the day, with 769 produced from 1928 to 1930.

Strange Flights

The Robin was a practical airplane, but best remembered for unusual flights. In 1929, Dale "Red" Jackson performed over four hundred slow rolls without stopping in his Robin. Later, Jackson and Forrest O'Brine spent nearly twenty-seven days circling over St. Louis. In 1935 their record was bettered by Fred and Al Key, who flew their Robin for 653 continuous hours—almost a month in the air! Fuel was delivered from another Robin, via hose, while mail, food, and spare parts came in a supply bag on the end of a rope. These endurance flights showed not only the reliability of the Robin, but the dependability of aircraft in general during the 1930s.

Douglas "Wrong Way" Corrigan

Experienced pilot and mechanic Douglas Corrigan told New Yorkers that he intended to set out for California on July 17, 1938, after he was denied permission to make a transatlantic flight. The next day he landed in Dublin, Ireland, becoming just the eighth person to cross the Atlantic alone. Corrigan, who had helped build Lindbergh's *Spirit of St. Louis*, had made the flight in a nine-year-old, secondhand Robin. Upon touching down after over twenty-eight hours, he became an international celebrity. Corrigan's explanation for his amazing flight: "I guess I made a mistake."

The Museum's Robin, dubbed *The Newsboy*, was purchased in 1929 by the *Daily Gazette* of McCook, Nebraska. It flew 380 miles a day (600 km) to deliver five thousand newspapers to forty towns in rural Nebraska. At each town, pilot Steve Tuttle would drop a bundle of newspapers out a hole in the bottom of the fuselage. *The Newsboy* was damaged in a tornado and sold, ending an unusual story in both journalism and aviation. The aircraft was loaned to the Museum in 1972.

Cessna CG-2 Glider

Manufacturer: Cessna
Model: CG-2 Glider
Year: 1930
Registration: N178V
Serial No.: 50

Span: 36.17 feet
Length: 18 feet
Height: 6.83 feet
Wing Area: 157 square feet
Weight: 120 pounds
Flying Speed: 25 mph
Landing Speed: 15 mph
Location: Museum of Flight
Viewable

Anyone Could Fly

In 1930, the Cessna Aircraft Company offered the public a chance to fly. For the price of $398, a CG-2 glider could be bought from a catalog. The CG design was based on German primary gliders used to train pilots after World War I. The CG could be pulled into the air by automobile or aircraft, or it could be launched to flight speed by a slingshot-like device off a hill or ridge.

To Survive the Great Depression

To keep his aircraft manufacturing company alive in hard times, Clyde Cessna began to sell small and simple aircraft such as the CG-2. Designed and built with his son, Eldon, the little sport glider became the basis for many other small Cessna aircraft including the CPG-1 (a powered glider), the CS-1 (a sailplane), and the EC-2 (a tiny one-place monoplane). Sadly, sales of the CG-2 and its offspring could not save the Cessna Company from closing for three years during the 1930s.

The Museum's CG-2 was purchased in 1930 by ten members of the Yakima Glider Club. The glider cost $400 and was flown for ten years by members of the club.

Stinson SR Reliant

Bushplane

The new 1933 Stinson SR was a bargain at the rock-bottom price of $3,995. It combined the best parts of earlier Stinson designs with a "man-sized" four-passenger cabin seen only in aircraft of twice the price. Months after its appearance, the Reliant was outselling all other two, four, and six-place cabin planes combined! During World War II, modified and more powerful Reliants flew with the British Royal Navy as the AT-19, while civilian Reliants were pressed into Army, Navy, and Royal Air Force service. After the war, Stinson SRs again became popular with American and Canadian sportsmen, businessmen, and bush pilots.

Off the Runway

Flying a plane equipped with skis or floats is different from flying a landplane. Operating from a snow-covered lake or summertime bay is a feat for the experienced flyer. Where else is the airfield an always-changing expanse where logs, or holes, or even fish appear on the "runway"? Fish you ask? If you fly from the water, sooner or later it will happen—a fish jumps from the water in the path of your onrushing plane on takeoff. If it's large enough, a fish can damage the propeller or break your windshield! Many seaplanes and "skiplanes" are equipped with tough metal propellers to minimize damage from all sorts of strange debris.

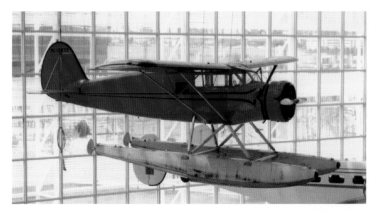

Flight Fact: Stinson's logo, a bow and arrow ready to shoot, faced upwards until the outbreak of World War II—when it was turned to face forwards.

The Museum's Stinson was built in 1933. It flew as a landplane with many pilots in the Northeast before being switched to twin-floats for water landings. Beginning in 1979, it flew in Alaska—sometimes equipped with skis.

Manufacturer: Stinson
Model: SR Reliant
Year: 1933
Registration: N13477
Serial No.: 8732

Span: 43.25 feet
Length: 27 feet
Height: 8.42 feet
Wing Area: 235 square feet
Empty Weight: 2070 pounds
Gross Weight: 3155 pounds
Cruise Speed: 115 mph
Service Ceiling: 14000 feet
Range: 460 miles
Location: Museum of Flight
Viewable

The Museum's Yakima Clipper has made over forty flights and has been part of the Museum's collection since 1987.

McAllister Yakima Clipper

Manufacturer: McAllister
Model: Yakima Clipper
Year: 1932
Registration: N10655
Serial No.: None

Span: 50.42 feet
Length: 21.5 feet
Wing Area: 164 square feet
Gross Weight: 352 pounds
Glide Ratio: 20-25 to 1
Location: Museum of Flight
Viewable

A World Record Attempt Over Washington

The Yakima Clipper was designed and built in 1931 and 1932 by Washington State native Charles McAllister. Based on German gliders he saw in a 1929 *National Geographic* article, the Yakima Clipper is made of wood with fabric-covered wings. With McAllister at the controls in June 1933, the sleek glider was flown in an attempt to break the world record for soaring endurance. After a Northwest record of eight hours and fifty-two minutes aloft, the wind abated and McAllister was forced to land short of the world record.

Charles McAllister: A Northwest First

Charles McAllister's Yakima Clipper was the first licensed glider in Washington. McAllister holds the state's first glider pilot's license and his first aviator's license was signed by Orville Wright. McAllister built his first glider from a 1918 *Popular Mechanics* article at age fifteen. In 1926, he formed McAllister's Flying School in Yakima, Washington, and he was a founding member of the Yakima Glider Club, established in 1930.

The Clipper

Charlie says that building the Yakima Clipper took two years. Made mostly of sitka spruce and plywood, he designed the fuselage tall and narrow, "so I could see better," Charlie says, "very safe, very sturdy." How sturdy? The wings each took 1,000 pounds (450 kg) of weight in load tests and bent about 3 feet (.9 m) with no signs of breakage. "In flight," comments McAllister, "I could never get them to bend over a foot." Flying the Yakima Clipper was tricky. Charlie says that without lots of flying experience, his first flight could have been a crash. "She had poor aileron control," says Charlie, who soon mastered the glider and logged around one hundred hours of flight time in it.

Flight Fact: The Yakima Clipper has been flown by only one pilot—Charlie himself.

Fairchild 24 W

Manufacturer: Fairchild
Model: 24 W
Year: 1941
Registration: N37161
Serial No.: 206

Span: 36.33 feet
Length: 23.75 feet
Height: 7.5 feet
Wing Area: 174.3 square feet
Empty Weight: 1524 pounds
Gross Weight: 2562 pounds
Cruise Speed: 120 mph
Max Speed: 134 mph
Service Ceiling: 15500 feet
Range: 720 miles
Location: Museum of Flight
Viewable

A Classic

The Fairchild F-24 is a truly classic aircraft in its field. Built in the 1930s and 1940s as an economical and easy to fly touring aircraft, the F-24 became the plane of choice for many Hollywood stars including Robert Taylor, Tyrone Power, Mary Pickford, and Jimmy Stewart. When the U.S. entered World War II, Fairchild's production line was diverted to the military and the F-24 became the Army UC-61 Forwarder light utility transport and the Royal Air Force Argus. Civilian versions of the planes were also pressed into service. After the war, the manufacturing rights were sold to Temco, which built 280 additional F-24s to bring the total number to about 1,800 planes.

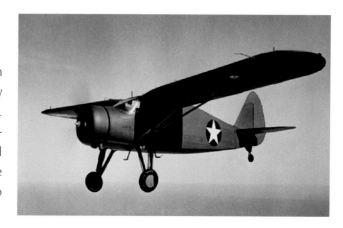

Sherman M. Fairchild

Sherman M. Fairchild's father was a New York congressmen and one of the founders of IBM. But the younger Fairchild's interest was photography. When he couldn't find a suitable platform for his invention, an aerial camera, he built the planes to carry them. Establishing Fairchild Aircraft Manufacturing Corporation in 1925, he later acquired Krieder-Reisner Aircraft Company. Growing and expanding, Fairchild ultimately was an empire of companies and divisions building airplanes, cameras, and aviation and space equipment. Sherman Fairchild was inducted into the National Aviation Hall of Fame in 1979.

Long-nosed Rs and Stubby Ws

Fairchild F-24s were produced with two different types of engines, which give each a distinctive appearance. Some, including the Museum's example, have Warner "Super Scarab" radial engines. These planes, called F-24Ws, have stubby noses housing the round engine with pistons oriented around a central crankshaft. The others, called F-24Rs, have Ranger in-line engines. These engines have their pistons in a line front-to-back and allow a more streamlined look to the long-nosed F-24R-versions.

Flight Fact: Fairchild's first F-24s, built in 1931, were two-seat aircraft. Additional seats were added to the design in 1934 and 1938, making it the four place aircraft we think of today.

The Museum's F-24 was built in Hagerstown, Maryland in early 1941 and purchased by famous ventriloquist Edgar Bergen. Bergen sold the plane to the president of a Spokane radio station and it was acquired for Army use in 1943. After the war, it flew with many private owners until it was purchased and restored by Ragnar Pettersson in 1981. Pettersson donated the F-24 to the Museum in 1985.

Piper J-3 Cub

Manufacturer: Piper
Model: J-3 Cub
Year: 1946
Registration: N88023
Serial No.: 15641

Span: 35.21 feet
Length: 22.38 feet
Height: 6.67 feet
Wing Area: 178.5 square feet
Empty Weight: 680 pounds
Gross Weight: 1220 pounds
Cruise Speed: 73 mph
Max Speed: 87 mph
Service Ceiling: 11500 feet
Range: 220 miles
Location: Museum of Flight
Viewable

Light Plane

The name Piper Cub is nearly synonymous with light plane. It was designed as a small, simple airplane for flight training. The J-3 first flew in 1937, but its lineage stretches back to the 1930 Taylor E-2 Cub. The J-3 Cub was popular in the pre-war years, but World War II thrust the little plane into a new role. The Army purchased 5,677 Cubs, called L-4s, for observation and liaison. Cubs, along with similar aircraft produced by Aeronca and Taylorcraft, enabled commanders to move quickly among their troops, spot from the air, and help direct artillery fire.

After the war, many Cubs returned to civilian life, where they helped to popularize aviation in the post-war period. Although production of the over fourteen thousand civilian J-3 Cubs ended in 1947, its descendants, most notably the Piper PA-18 Super Cub, were manufactured into the 1990s.

William Thomas Piper, Sr. (1881-1970)

William Piper entered aviation in 1929 by investing in the Taylor Brothers Aircraft Corporation. A year later, the Taylor Model E-2 Cub was built. By 1937, Piper had bought out the Taylors' interest in the company and established the Piper Aircraft Corporation. The Piper Cub, Cub Coupe, and Cruiser soon followed. Before he retired in 1968, Piper's company developed a long line of general aviation planes, including the Comanche, Cherokee, Aztec, and Navaho. Piper was inducted into the National Aviation Hall of Fame in 1980 for his development, production, and marketing of the light plane for general aviation, military, and commercial use.

Aerocar III

Manufacturer: Aerocar
Model: Model III
Year: 1968
Registration: N100D
Serial No.: 1

Span: 34 feet
Length: 26 feet
Wing Area: 190 square feet
Empty Weight: 1500 pounds
Gross Weight: 2100 pounds
Cruise Speed (Road): 60 mph
Cruise Speed (Air): 135 mph
Service Ceiling: 12000 feet
Range: 500 miles
Location: Museum of Flight
Viewable

A Plane in Every Garage

After World War II many people envisioned an airplane in every garage in America's expanding suburbs. One of these visions took the form of Moulton Taylor's Aerocar. The Aerocar was a "roadable" airplane—certified for use as both a plane and an automobile. The prototype was completed in 1949 but not certified by the Civil Aeronautics Administration until 1956. Taylor came close to producing his car with both Ling-Temco-Vought and Ford but both deals fell through.

A Flying Automobile

Of course, the most remarkable feature of the Aerocar is its ability to transform from automobile to aircraft—a process that takes about fifteen minutes. On the ground, the Aerocar can either tow its wings and tail like a trailer, or simply leave them at the airport.

To get ready for flight, the driver/pilot first connects the drive shaft (flip up the license plate to make the connection) in the tail. Then, the wings swing around into position and get pinned into place. The flight controls—movable steering wheel and rudder pedals—slide into place automatically. The engine cannot start unless every connection has been properly made—an ingenious safety device.

Thanks to its large airplane engine, the Aerocar was quite sporty and by all accounts it was also quite stable and pleasant to fly.

Flight Fact: The Aerocar III's brother, the Aerocar II, was not a car at all. It was built as a non-roadable, four place airplane designed by Taylor.

The Museum's Aerocar III began as the sixth and final Aerocar I. In the late 1960s it was damaged in a road accident and Taylor bought it back. He updated and redesigned the car section leaving the wings essentially unchanged.

Bowers Fly Baby

EAA Contest Winner

The Fly Baby was the winning entry in the 1962 Experimental Aircraft Association (EAA) Design Contest. Developed by Seattle resident Peter Bowers, the little plane specifically met the EAA's requirements for a low-cost, folding wing plane that could be towed or trailered, and is easy to build and fly. Still a popular design with many homebuilt aircraft enthusiasts, the Fly Baby's plans sell for about $65. The finished airplane can fit in a standard garage and can also be built in biplane and twin-float seaplane versions.

Peter M. Bowers

Seattle resident Peter Bowers wrote his first aviation article as a high school student in 1938. Today, he is one of the world's most respected aviation historians with numerous books and hundreds of articles to his credit. Bowers built a replica Curtiss Pusher, which he flew at air shows, as well as the prototype of his own design—the award-winning Fly Baby.

Flight Fact: Although not intended for heavy acrobatics, the little Flybaby can do simple loops, barrel rolls, and spins.

The Museum's plane was built by Al Stabler, who gave an overview in his aircraft log of how the Museum's Fly Baby was built. He purchased the plans in November 1967, beginning actual work early in 1968. The all-wood construction consisted of spruce structural members, fir plywood, and mahogany door skins. The gas tank and engine cowling were homemade and the wheels, propeller, and engine were purchased

locally. The airframe was inspected by the FAA in September 1970 and the registration number was assigned. Soon after, the wings were covered with Ceconite 101 fabric and nine coats of brushed-on dope. That November, Al began taxi tests and on February 2, 1971 at Kitsap County Airport, his Fly Baby finally took to the skies in its maiden flight! The plane was retired in 1980 with about 130 hours of flying time.

Manufacturer: Bowers
Model: Fly Baby
Year: 1962
Registration: N4339
Serial No.: 68-15

Span: 28 feet
Length: 18.5 feet
Height (wings folded): 6.5 feet
Wing Area: 120 square feet
Empty Weight: 605 pounds
Gross Weight: 924 pounds
Cruise Speed: 105 to 110 mph
Max Speed: 120 mph
Service Ceiling: 15000 feet
Range: 320 miles
Location: Museum of Flight
Viewable

Eipper Cumulus VB

Manufacturer: Eipper
Model: Cumulus VB
Year: 1975
Registration: None
Serial No.: None

Span: 29.5 feet
Length: 13.17 feet
Wing Area: 165 square feet
Weight: 41 pounds
Glide Ratio: 7 to 1
Min. Sink Rate: 250 feet per minute
Materials: Aluminum and Dacron
Location: Museum of Flight
Viewable

On the Winds of Change

In 1976 the Eipper Cumulus could be purchased for $950, and it offered a simple, light, and portable hang glider with high performance. An ongoing design program since 1974, the VB version had a superior sink rate and glide angle to many of its competitors and began winning contests throughout the world in late 1975.

The Museum's small and light Eipper glider was purchased by William Becker and carries all eleven of the colors available for the sail. It was first flown near Point Fermin, California and was donated to the Museum of Flight in 1983.

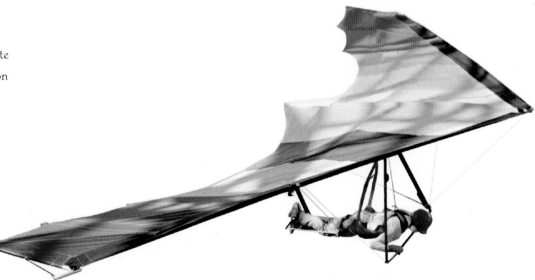

Stephens Akro

Manufacturer: Stephens
Model: Akro
Year: 1970
Registration: N78JN
Serial No.: 434

Wing Span: 24.5 feet
Length: 19.08 feet
Height: 5.67 feet
Wing Area: 94 square feet
Empty Weight: 850 pounds
Max. Weight: 1200 pounds
Cruise Speed: 145 mph
Max Speed: 225 mph
Service Ceiling: 22000 feet
Location: Museum of Flight
Viewable

Spunky Stunt Plane

Clayton Stephens designed the Akro specifically for homebuilders who wanted a plane for competitive aerobatics. The late Margaret Ritchie, 1966 U.S. Women's Aerobatic Champion, flew the prototype. The Akro's wooden wings and fabric-covered steel tube fuselage might seem flimsy, but it's rated to +12g and -11g—meaning the plane can withstand the violent stresses of aerobatic maneuvers.

Her Other Plane Is a 767

The Akro aerobatic plane was an air show favorite with Seattle native Joann Osterud at the controls. Joann learned to fly at Boeing Field in Seattle, Washington, and now performs magnificent maneuvers like hammerhead turns, tail-slides, and *lomcevaks* (tumbling end over end) on the air show circuit. Osterud also has a second aviation career—she was the first woman pilot hired by Alaska Airlines and currently flies Boeing 767s for United Airlines.

The Museum's Akro was built by Gary Zimmerman, and in 1971, became the first amateur-built Akro to fly. Purchased by Joann Osterud in 1976, the plane is a veteran of hundreds of aerobatic performances. Osterud donated the Akro to the Museum in 1994.

Lamson Alcor

Manufacturer: Lamson
Model: L106 Alcor
Year: 1972
Registration: N924LR
Serial No.: 18

Span: 66 feet
Length: 25 feet
Height: 6 feet
Wing Area: 154 square feet
Empty Weight: 600 pounds
Gross Weight: 950 pounds
Top Speed: 140 mph
Operational Ceiling: 25000 feet
Location: Museum of Flight
Viewable

An Unconventional Sailplane

The Alcor, conceived during the early 1960s by Robert Lamson, was one of the first sailplanes in the U.S. made of composite materials. Today, similar materials have taken an ever more prominent role in the aviation industry. Other innovations, like a pressurized cockpit (a first for a sailplane) and a solar heater, keep the Alcor's pilot comfortable at high altitudes. Lamson flew the experimental sailplane recreationally from 1973 until it was donated for use in a scientific study.

From 1985 to 1989, the Alcor flew in a study of the Chinook Arch in Alberta, Canada. The Chinook Arch is a weather phenomenon associated with severe turbulence in the Canadian Rockies. Unlike powered aircraft, the Alcor could glide over the area of interest and collect undisturbed meteorological and environmental data for extended periods of time.

Robert Lamson

Alcor designer and builder Robert Lamson turned his interest in composite technology at the University of Washington into a fifty-year career in aviation. After a brief period in the Army Air Corps, Lamson joined the Boeing Aircraft Company as a test pilot. During the 1940s, he worked at Boeing on oxygen systems for high-altitude flight, leading to his interest in aircraft pressurization. Since 1952, Lamson has worked as an aviation consultant.

Composite Construction: N924LR, 18

Lamson's interest in composite construction led to the innovative design of the Alcor. The sailplane's fuselage consists of sitka spruce veneers over-wrapped with fiberglass; foam sandwich assemblies over S glass monospars were used for the wings and tail. This construction allowed for an airframe that was light, yet very strong. These materials also had an interesting side effect—the wings bent upwards in flight. Although this might be a bit disconcerting to some, it actually has aerodynamic benefits that improved performance.

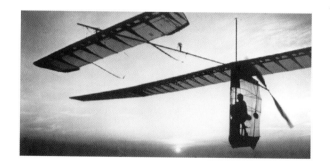

Gossamer Albatross II

Manufacturer: MacCready
Model: Gossamer Albatross II
Year: 1979
Registration: None
Serial No.: GA-II

Span: 97.67 feet
Length: 34 feet
Height: 16 feet
Wing Area: 488 square feet
Empty Weight: 70 pounds
Gross Weight: 215 pounds
Max Speed: 18 mph
Range: 35 miles
Location: Museum of Flight
Viewable

Human-Powered Marvel

The Gossamer Albatross aircraft is designed to fly long distances with a human as the only power source. This light and fragile aircraft is pushed by a propeller connected, through a series of gears, to a constantly pedaling pilot. On June 12, 1979, the Albatross, powered and guided by pilot Bryan Allen, made an historic flight across the English Channel. The record-breaking flight covered a distance of 22.25 miles (35.6 km) in two hours and forty-nine minutes.

The Albatross II later took part in NASA-funded low speed stability tests and was the first human-powered aircraft to make a controlled flight inside an enclosed structure—the Houston Astrodome.

It Flies Backwards!

As a boy, Paul MacCready was always interested in unorthodox aircraft. He designed and built many model planes with the horizontal stabilizer forward of the wing. This canard-type configuration was common in the early days of aviation—even the Wright brothers built their Flyer that way. MacCready's award-winning Gossamer Albatross retains this pioneering design characteristic.

How Is It Made?

The Albatross is an almost all-plastic machine. Its skeleton is made of the same type of carbon-fiber tubing used in golf club shafts and fishing rods. It's strong, more than three times stronger than aluminum, and only about half as heavy. The ribs and leading edges of the wings are made of polystyrene foam and the whole structure is covered with a Mylar film. The only metal parts on the plane are the pedals, cranks, drive chain, seat post, and a few fittings and wires.

The Albatross II on display at the Museum was built as a backup to the Albatross aircraft that flew across the Channel. Except for some minor design changes, this craft is identical to the record-breaking Albatross.

Lear Fan 2100

Manufacturer: Lear Fan
Model: 2100
Year: 1980
Registration: N626BL
Serial No.: 1

Span: 39.33 feet
Length: 40.58 feet
Height: 12.17 feet
Empty Weight: 4100 pounds
Takeoff Weight: 7350 pounds
Cruise Speed: 322 mph
Max Speed: 425 mph
Service Ceiling: 41000 feet
Range: 1548 miles
Location: Museum of Flight
Viewable

Corporate PropJet

The Lear Fan 2100, a radical two-engine pusher prop-jet made almost entirely from composites, was Bill Lear's final project. When Lear died before his marvel of aviation technology became a reality, his widow, Moya, and Lear's employees honored his final wish to finish and fly the airplane.

As a testament to the efforts to complete the aircraft by its 1980 deadline, the British government, which helped fund the project, declared the Lear Fan's first flight date "December 32, 1980." Envelopes carried aboard the flight were cancelled with this same date, and the U.S. Post Office honored the cancellation.

Father of the "Bizjet"

In 1959, when word leaked out that William Lear was going to build a small, six-passenger jet plane, critics snickered. "There's no market for that!" they said, "Who's gonna buy it?" In 1964, his Learjet, based partly on a Swiss fighter design, set off a revolution in business aviation. Today, Lear's name is synonymous with the executive jet.

The Composite Craft

The Lear Fan is unique because it is made almost entirely of graphite/epoxy and Kevlar composite materials. These composites make the Lear Fan strong at about half the weight of an aluminum airframe. The lighter Lear Fan is faster and more economical than conventionally made business jets and turboprops. Only three Lear Fans were made, but the knowledge gained in composite technology has revolutionized the field of aviation.

The Museum's model—the prototype—made its maiden flight in January 1981.

Insitu Aerosonde

Manufacturer: Insitu
Model: Aerosonde
Year: 1998
Registration: None
Serial No.: None

Span: 9.67 feet
Length: 5.67 feet
Height: 2 feet
Wing Area: 6.1 square feet
Gross Weight: 28.9 pounds
Cruise Speed: 43 to 55 mph
Service Ceiling: 15000 feet
Range: 1875 miles
Location: Museum of Flight
Viewable

Robotic Flyer

This little plane set a record by flying across the Atlantic without a pilot—seventy-one years after Lindberg h's historic solo. Incredibly, it took more than a day and less than two gallons of gas! Called an Aerosonde, it's powered by a modified model airplane engine and is designed to head out to sea and report on the weather. Aerosondes carry a small computer, meteorological instruments, and a GPS (Global Positioning System) receiver to navigate.

Airborne Weatherman

Aerosondes are designed to collect data over the ocean where weather stations are few and far between. Their measurements of temperature, pressure, humidity, and wind within the atmosphere complement the "big picture" data provided by satellites. Someday Aerosondes may circulate regularly on weather-reconnaissance flights between Hawaii, Alaska, and the mainland. The information they gather will often allow improved weather forecasting for the West Coast.

The Museum's Aerosonde is nicknamed *Laima* after the ancient Latvian deity of good fortune. On August 21, 1998, after more than twenty-six hours in stormy skies, *Laima* finished the history-making 2,044-mile (3270 km) flight from Newfoundland to an island off Scotland.

Commercial Aircraft

The Boeing 747 is so big that it has been said that it does not fly; the earth merely drops out from under it.

— *Captain Ned Wilson, Pan Am*

Alan Mulally

In 2001, Seattle's Museum of Flight was invited to send its flag into space aboard a Space Shuttle mission. Traveling with the flag was the following description:

Aviation began as a dream, born of wonder and curiosity. The dream became a theory through imagination and intelligence. The theory became an experiment through courage and study. The experiment became a practice through vision and learning. This progression has been a profound adventure, an awakening of the human soul to the possibilities of dreams.

To me, that summarizes the magic of flight and the spirit that has attracted many of us to want to dedicate our lives to contributing to the world's commercial aviation industry.

Look at how far we have come in such a relatively short period of time. The Wright brothers' first flight at Kitty Hawk, North Carolina, on Dec. 17, 1903, could have been performed within the 150-foot economy section of today's 747-400. From wood, wire and linen cloth beginnings to, as they say, four million parts flying in close formation. The Wright brothers' success gave the world an inkling of the very real possibilities that were within reach. It didn't take long for things to snowball. Only a few short years later a variety of new, improved aircraft and airplane manufacturing companies began to appear. An industry was born.

Air transportation is widely considered to be the second greatest single contributor to economic development, behind education. The profound and fundamental changes in our world during the last century have been significantly influenced by commercial aviation. It has affected everything from our methods of worldwide commerce to leisure.

Commercial aviation links people worldwide as they had never been linked before. Point-to-point service, improvements in passenger comfort, increased frequency, and lower fares continue to make commercial air travel attractive and available to more people around the world. With increased airplane range and performance, passengers are able to go where they want, when they want, and how they want more than ever before. And, at the end of the day, that's what commercial aviation is all about: getting people together. It is a very powerful and special endeavor. Because when we get people together barriers break down, communication and knowledge exchange takes place, and good things happen more often than not.

The Boeing Company has had the good fortune and privilege to be involved in the development of a wide variety of commercial aircraft that have helped to change the world. Each day we join the world's other aerospace companies in the constant pursuit of the dream of flight by designing and building airplanes that push the boundaries of speed, comfort and economic efficiency. The past 100 years of commercial aviation have clearly shown that we can accomplish difficult tasks, many of which were once thought to be impossible. This has happened so many times that the future of flight has to be considered limitless.

These pages show a legacy of tremendous human achievement in commercial flight. Visionary leaders. Brilliant people. Great companies. Amazing technology. Historic milestones. And, as always with commercial air travel, the best is yet to come.

—*Alan Mulally*, President and CEO, Boeing Commercial Airplanes

Manufacturer: Boeing
Model: B & W
Year: 1916
Registration: N1916
Serial No.: 1A – Replica

Span: 52 feet
Length: 31.17 feet
Wing Area: 580 square feet
Empty Weight: 2100 pounds
Gross Weight: 2800 pounds
Max Speed: 75 mph
Range: 320 miles
Location: Museum of Flight
Viewable

The First Boeing

The B & W was the first airplane designed and built by Boeing. On June 15, 1916, Mr. Boeing himself took the B & W aloft for the first time. Later, Boeing showed the plane to the Navy in hopes of a contract but was turned down. Both the first B & W, nicknamed *Bluebill*, and the second, built the following November, were eventually acquired by the government of New Zealand.

Boeing and Westervelt

Prominent timber man William E. Boeing met a Navy engineer named Conrad Westervelt at Seattle's University Club. He found that they had similar interests—both bachelors liked boating and bridge, had studied engineering, and shared a fascination with the dawning field of aviation. On July 4, 1914, they arranged for their first flight in a Curtiss seaplane. They were impressed, but both men agreed that they could build a better airplane. The result was the B & W, named with the initials of its creators.

One Better

The B & W's basic design was derived from a Martin T.A. Trainer that Mr. Boeing had purchased after taking flying lessons at Glenn Martin's school in Los Angeles. As he honed his flying skills with the seaplane, Boeing's creative mind raced ahead, figuring improvements and innovations that he would incorporate into the B & W. The most important changes were a lighter, improved aerodynamic wing section and twin pontoon configuration that gave the B & W better and safer landings.

Flight Fact: A young pilot and mechanic named Herb Munter was Boeing's first employee. Munter was supposed to pilot the B & W on its first flight. When Munter was late, Boeing decided he couldn't wait and test flew the plane himself.

The Museum's B & W is a 1966 replica built for The Boeing Company's 50th anniversary. Though externally similar to the original B & W, it incorporates a number of design changes for safety and ease of construction, such as revised tail surfaces, steel-tube fuselage, and a different engine.

Swallow Commercial

Manufacturer: Swallow
Model: Commercial
Year: 1927
Registration: N6070
Serial No.: 968

Span: 32.67 feet
Length: 23.83 feet
Height: 8.92 feet
Wing Area: 300 square feet
Empty Weight: 1447 pounds
Gross Weight: 2200 pounds
Cruise Speed: 85 mph
Max Speed: 100 mph
Range: 450 miles
Location: Museum of Flight
Viewable

Pasco to Elko

In 1925, the Post Office began to make contracts with private operators to carry mail. One route—from Pasco, Washington to Elko, Nevada—called CAM 5, was awarded to Walter T. Varney. Varney acquired six new Swallows for the dangerous route over the mountains and desert. Varney soon found that the Swallows were underpowered, and larger Wright J-4 engines were installed. Later, Varney Air Lines and other companies including Boeing Air Transport, merged to become United Air Lines.

Starting an Airline

How was an airline started in 1926? First, Varney had one of his Swallows shipped to Elko. There, the new airline's chief pilot, Leon Cuddeback, assembled the plane and took it for a flight. "To make sure it would get over the mountains in the area," he later explained. Meanwhile, since there were no maps of the route, Varney toured the landscape by motorcar, sketching a map onto a postcard.

The rest of the Swallows went to Boise—the route's halfway point. When two pilots sent to arrange the flight from Pasco crashed on landing and broke their noses, Cuddeback unexpectedly found that he would pilot the first Swallow from Pasco. On April 6, 1926, five hundred residents of Pasco came to see pilot Leon Cuddeback and the first mail-laden Swallow take off for Elko via Boise, Idaho.

One Rough Route

CAM 5 involved some of the highest and roughest terrain in the country. When asked about the route's chances for success, General Billy Mitchell commented, "If they knew what they were trying to do, they wouldn't even start it." But Varney did, and Cuddeback's first flight was a great success. And the second? Franklin Rose took off from Elko on the return flight, got off course, and crash-landed. Two days later the downed pilot, carrying his sack of mail, managed to locate a phone to tell Varney he was alive. CAM 5 was one rough route.

Flight Fact: The new Swallow was designed by Lloyd Stearman, who started his own aircraft company in 1926. Stearman's brother, Waverly, redesigned the Swallow in 1927.

The Museum's plane is a 1928 Swallow Commercial or "OX-5 Swallow" restored to look like a Varney Swallow Mail Plane. It was flown by Buck Hilbert for United Air Lines' 50th anniversary.

The Museum's M-1 is thought to be the first Ryan airframe built. It was abandoned in 1932 after it overturned during an emergency landing in Paso Robles, California. Recovered in 1980, it was restored by Ty Sundstrom.

Ryan M-1

Manufacturer: Ryan
Model: M-1
Year: 1926
Registration: N46853
Serial No.: HN-1

Span: 36 feet
Length: 24 feet
Height: 8 feet 2 in
Wing Area: 227.5 square feet
Empty Weight: 1550 pounds
Gross Weight: 2700 pounds
Cruise Speed: 110 mph
Max Speed: 125 mph
Service Ceiling: 15000 feet
Range: 400 miles
Location: Museum of Flight
Viewable

Ryan's First Plane

Airmail kept the post-war aviation industry alive in the U.S. In 1925, Congress privatized the airmail business and private carriers replaced Post Office flyers. The Ryan M-1, dubbed "the plane that pays a profit," was America's first production monoplane and, starting on September 15, 1926, the first commercial plane to fly with Pacific Air Transport (PAT) along the West Coast. PAT's six M-1s linked Seattle, Portland, San Francisco, and Los Angeles. The cost was high—five of PAT's original M-1s crashed the first year. PAT was sold to Boeing Air Transport in 1928.

The M-1's Big Little Brother—Lindbergh's Plane

Does this plane look familiar? The M-1 has traits of another famous Ryan aircraft—the *Spirit of St. Louis*. Charles Lindbergh came to Ryan in 1927 and flew an M-1. He requested a similar but larger plane to make the non-stop 3,600-mile (5,760 km) flight across the Atlantic. Ryan's M-1 design was modified to fit Lindbergh's requirements. The *Spirit of St. Louis*, built as the Ryan NYP (New York-Paris), was completed in just sixty days. Total price—$10,580.

The Man Who Built the Company

The days after Lindbergh's famous flight were bittersweet for T. Claude Ryan, who was the founder of Ryan Airlines, Inc. and the creative influence behind the M-1. Mr. Ryan had sold his interest in the company that bore his name to Frank Mahoney, his partner, just six months before "Lucky Lindy" landed in Paris. As the Ryan name appeared in newspapers around the globe and Lindbergh sung the praises of his trusty Ryan airplane, Mr. Ryan sat on the sideline, merely a manager in the company he helped build.

Flight Fact: Five M-1s were sold to a man who planned to use them for a revolution in Mexico. They were impounded by a U.S. Attorney and eventually resold.

Alexander Eaglerock

Manufacturer: Alexander
Model: Eaglerock Combo-Wing
Year: 1928
Registration: N4648
Serial No.: 469

Span: 36 feet
Length: 24.92 feet
Height: 9.92 feet
Wing Area: 330 square feet
Empty Weight: 1420 pounds
Gross Weight: 2180 pounds
Cruise Speed: 85 mph
Max Speed: 100 mph
Range: 395 miles
Location: Museum of Flight
Viewable

Replacing the World War I "Crates"

The Alexander Eaglerock was one of a number of airplanes that were built for civilian use to replace the dwindling supplies of World War I surplus craft. Winging away from the Denver-based Alexander Company at "mile-high" altitudes, the Eaglerock cruised at heights and speeds that many old and weary warplanes couldn't reach anymore.

Too Much Ahead of Its Time?

In 1925, the first Eaglerock bristled with innovations such as a tail wheel and wings that folded back. When buyers didn't seem ready for such modern gimmicks, a more conventional plane appeared in early 1926. The Eaglerock is considered one of the first significant certified aircraft, with ATC (Approved Type Certificate) #7 assigned to the Combo-wing and ATC #8 to the Long-wing version on April 27, 1927.

Frank and Victor Hansen purchased the Museum of Flight's Eaglerock in 1977. "It was a basket case," Victor says. "We probably wouldn't have restored the plane if it hadn't been for Dad." Their father had owned an Eaglerock in the 1920s. He barnstormed with the plane until a crash left it in tatters. "He had no money during the Great Depression," Frank relates, "So even though he loved the plane, he couldn't fix it." The Hansens, with Bill Duncan, restored this Eaglerock in their father's honor.

The Museum's C-3B was acquired in 1986 when it was flown into Boeing Field from Prosser, Washington. It was built in February 1928 and has been restored as a Western Air Express airmail carrier by R. J. McWhorter. Western Air Express began flying C-3Bs in late 1927.

Stearman C-3B

Manufacturer: Stearman
Model: C-3B
Year: 1928
Registration: N7550
Serial No.: 166

Span: 35 feet
Length: 24 feet
Height: 9 feet
Wing Area: 297 square feet
Empty Weight: 1625 pounds
Gross Weight: 2650 pounds
Cruise Speed: 108 mph
Service Ceiling: 18000 feet
Range: 620 miles
Location: Museum of Flight
Viewable

Dynamo

When Varney Air Lines wanted to switch to a more powerful mail plane, they turned to Stearman. Known for rugged dependability and no-nonsense design, Stearman C-2s and C-3s became popular replacement planes on the short-haul "feeder" lines of America's growing commercial airmail system. The majority of Stearman C-3s were the C-3B Sport Commercial variety, with a Wright J-5 engine. Many C-3Bs were used as sport planes and advanced trainers well into the 1930s. Nearing the end of their days, some C-3s became crop-dusting aircraft until after World War II, when they were often replaced with another Stearman biplane—surplus Kaydet trainers.

Lloyd Stearman

Aeronautical engineer Lloyd Carlton Stearman worked for many aircraft companies early in his career. Laird Airplane Company, Swallow Aircraft Company, and Travel Air Manufacturing Company all had Stearman on their payroll before he established his own company in Venice, California in 1926. Stearman Aircraft, with the C-series of biplanes, became a direct competitor with Stearman's former employer—Travel Air. He not only designed the planes and supervised their construction, he also served as test pilot.

Hitting the Skids

Airplanes like the C-3B and the Swallow Commercial hanging beside it weren't built with tail wheels—they had skids. Before World War II, there weren't many paved airfields, they were actually fields—grass and dirt. Planes didn't have brakes and the tail skid, usually made of ash wood with a steel shoe, helped them stop. Taxiing with a brake always on might seem like a "drag," but there was minimum taxiing at old airfields. You just pointed the plane into the wind and you were off! The trusty skid kept you going somewhat straight until you gained speed to soar.

Flight Fact: A Stearman C-3B cost $8,970 in the late 1920s.

Boeing 80A-1

Manufacturer: Boeing
Model: 80A-1
Year: 1929
Registration: N224M
Serial No.: 1082

Span: 80 feet
Length: 56.5 feet
Height: 15.25 feet
Wing Area: 1220 square feet
Empty Weight: 10582 pounds
Gross Weight: 17500 pounds
Max Speed: 138 mph
Service Ceiling: 14000 feet
Range: 460 miles
Location: Museum of Flight
Viewable

Pioneer "Pullman" of the Air

Until the mid-1920s, American commercial airplanes were built for mail, people were secondary. Boeing's Model 80, along with the Ford and Fokker tri-motors, were a new breed of passenger aircraft. The advent of the Model 80 brought some comfort to travel with room for twelve, a heated cabin, and leather seats. There were individual reading lights and the lavatory featured hot and cold running water. Although the 80 had a luxurious interior, flying was tough by today's standards—the cabin wasn't pressurized, engine noise made conversation difficult, and despite heaters, the cabin was sometimes very cold. The twelve-passenger Model 80 and the more-powerful eighteen-passenger 80A (re-designated 80A-1 when the tail surfaces were modified in 1930) stayed in service until 1933, when replaced by the all-metal Boeing Model 247.

Stewardesses

In 1930, Miss Ellen Church, a student pilot and registered nurse, convinced Boeing management to hire female cabin attendants for their Model 80 flights. Until then, it had been the co-pilot's duty to pass out box lunches, serve coffee, and tend to the passengers' needs. Church reasoned that the sight of women working aboard the Boeing 80s would alleviate the passenger's fear of air travel. She and seven others, all nurses, became America's first stewardesses. Serving on a trial basis, they were very popular and became a permanent part of American commercial aviation

Flight Fact: Unlike the other passenger planes of the era, the Model 80 was a biplane. This design feature enabled it to have a slow landing speed at the high-altitude airports along Boeing Air Transport's San Francisco to Chicago route.

The Museum's Model 80A-1 was retired from service with United Air Lines in 1934. In 1941, it became a cargo aircraft with a construction firm in Alaska. To carry large pieces of equipment, including a massive 11,000-pound (4,950 kg) boiler, a cargo door was cut into the aircraft's side. After World War II, this plane was stored and then discarded. It was recovered from a dump in 1960 and eventually brought to Seattle for restoration. It is the only surviving example of the Boeing Model 80 series.

Boeing 247 D

Manufacturer: Boeing
Model: Model 247D
Year: 1934
Registration: N13347
Serial No.: 1729

Span: 74 feet
Length: 51.58 feet
Height: 12.15 feet
Wing Area: 836.13 square feet
Empty Weight: 9144 pounds
Gross Weight: 13650 pounds
Cruise Speed: 189 mph
Max Speed: 200 mph
Service Ceiling: 25400 feet
Range: 745 miles
Location: Restoration Center
(Everett, WA)
Viewable

A New Era for Air Travel

The first modern airliner, the Boeing 247 was developed in 1933, marking the beginning of a new era. Versatile, easy to maneuver, and economical to operate, the 247 quickly outshone other transports of the period. It was a metal, twin-engine airplane that carried ten passengers and sported new developments: an autopilot, pneumatically operated de-icing equipment, a variable-pitch propeller, and retractable landing gear.

Competition

United Air Lines, which had a monopoly on Boeing's production of 247s, was soon outdistancing its competition. This forced TWA to go to Douglas Aircraft to request a new plane that could compete—even outperform—the 247. The result of this challenge was the development of one of the most significant planes in aviation history—the Douglas DC-3.

Flight Fact: The 247s remained in airline service until World War II, when several were converted into C-73 transports and trainers.

One of only four known to exist today, the Museum's 247D is the only one still flying.

Douglas DC-2

Manufacturer: Douglas
Model: DC-2
Year: 1934
Registration: N1934D
Serial No.: 1368

Span: 85 feet
Length: 61.98 feet
Height: 16.31 feet

Wing Area: 939 square feet
Empty Weight: 12408 pounds
Gross Weight: 18560 pounds
Cruise Speed: 190 mph
Max Speed: 210 mph
Service Ceiling: 22450 feet
Range: 1000 miles
Location: Storage
Not Viewable

Douglas Does It Again

The DC-2 was an instant hit. It was similar in shape to the DC-1 but had more powerful engines, was faster and capable of longer flights. More importantly, it was two feet longer and could carry two more passengers. In its first six months of service, the DC-2 established nineteen American speed and distance records. In 1934, TWA put DC-2s on overnight flights called The Sky Chief from New York to Los Angeles. The flight left New York at 4 P.M. and, after stops in Chicago, Kansas City and Albuquerque, arrived in Los Angeles at 7 A.M. For the first time, the air traveler could fly from coast to coast without losing the business day.

Taking the Race

The DC-2 was the first Douglas airliner to enter service with an airline outside the United States. In October 1934, KLM Royal Dutch Airlines entered one of its DC-2s in the London-to-Melbourne air race. It made every scheduled passenger-stop on KLM's regular 9,000 mile route (1,000 miles longer than the official race route), carried mail, and even turned back once to pick up a stranded passenger. Yet the DC-2 finished in second place behind a racing plane built especially for the competition. After that, the DC-2's reputation was assured and it became the airplane of choice for many of the world's largest airlines.

In 1935, the DC-2 became the first Douglas aircraft to receive the prestigious Collier Trophy for outstanding achievements in flight. Between 1934 and 1937, Douglas built 156 DC-2s at its Santa Monica, California plant.

Antonov An-2

Manufacturer: Antonov
Model: An-2
Year: 1977
Registration: N61SL
Serial No.: 1G17527

Span: 59.71 feet
Length: 46.2 feet
Height: 13.77 feet
Wing Area: 765.3 square feet
Gross Weight: 12125 pounds
Cruise Speed: 124 mph
Max Speed: 157 mph
Service Ceiling: 14270 feet
Range: 562 miles
Location: Pearson Air Museum
Vancouver, WA
Viewable

Kolkhoznik Means "Collective Farmer"

Nearly 12,000 Antonov An-2 aircraft have been constructed since it was first designed in Russia in 1947. After initial production, construction was transferred to PZL in Poland. China was also licensed to build the aircraft. The largest single engine biplane to enter series production, the Antonov An-2, has a 59-foot wingspan, a four-bladed propeller, and a huge 1,000-hp engine. It helped fill the need for a simple, relatively low-cost, load-carrying, utility aircraft. Besides its use as a paratrooper transport, the aircraft has been used as an aerial ambulance and an agricultural sprayer. Its slow landing speed of approximately 45 mph and convertibility from wheels to snow skis or floats enables it to land in a variety of climates on open outback areas with makeshift airfields.

The Museum's An-2 is a 1977 Polish Antonov An-2, donated by owner Shane Lundgren and financed by Air Berlin airlines. Pembroke Capital, an aircraft leasing company, supported the plane's delivery from Ireland. In 1998, Lundgren used this Antonov to recreate the first west to east flight over the Arctic Ocean by George Hubert Wilkins and Carl Ben Eielson, who made the trip in 1928 in a Lockheed Vega from Point Barrow, Alaska, to Spitsbergen, Norway. During the reenactment, Lundgren's crew landed at the North Pole. The Boeing Company helped sponsor the trip.

Douglas DC-3

Manufacturer: Douglas
Model: DC-3
Year: 1940
Registration: N138D
Serial No.: 2245

Span: 95 feet
Length: 64.5 feet
Height: 16.92 feet
Wing Area: 987 square feet
Empty Weight: 16600 pounds
Gross Weight: 25200 pounds
Cruise Speed: 194 mph
Range: 2125 miles
Location: Museum of Flight
Viewable

Faithful "Gooney Bird"

The first versions of the DC-3, called Douglas Sleeper Transports, began service with American Airlines in 1936. Demand for the airliner was high because there was nothing directly comparable—by 1938, DC-3s were flying 95 percent of the United States' airline traffic. During World War II, the DC-3 design became a troop and cargo carrier called the C-47. Douglas built a total of 10,654 of the rugged and reliable planes and many are still flying today.

Donald Wills Douglas (1892-1981)

Engineer Donald Douglas created his own company in 1920. His Cloudster was the first aircraft to lift a payload equal to its own weight and the Douglas World Cruisers were the first to fly around the world. The Douglas name became associated with commercial transport through the Douglas Commercial or "DC-" series, including the DC-3. During wartime, Douglas built transports, bombers, and attack airplanes. Donald Douglas was inducted into the National Aviation Hall of Fame in 1969 for his design of both military and commercial aircraft.

The Museum's DC-3 was built in 1940 for American Airlines. It has seen service with various airlines and has flown over 20,000 hours. It now wears the livery of Alaska Airlines, which operated many DC-3s and C-47s after World War II.

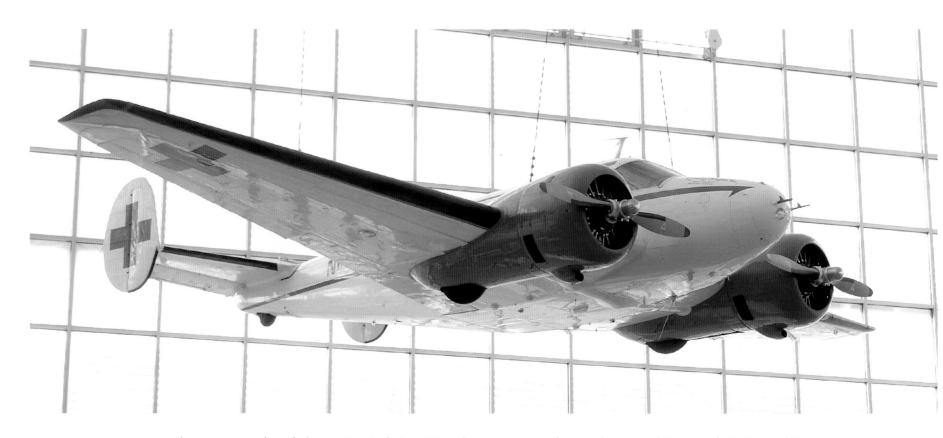

The Museum's Beech was built in 1942 and rebuilt in 1951. After seventeen years of serving the Army and Air Force, the C-45 was sold to Mercy Flights, Inc., based in Medford, Oregon. Nicknamed Iron Annie and The Bandaid Bomber, the C-45 evacuated over 1,150 people from remote areas in Oregon and northern California to city hospitals for medical care. This plane also flew missions to locate downed aircraft and assisted in firefighting operations before being retired in 1980.

Beech C-45H

Manufacturer: Beech
Model: C-45H
Year: 1942
Registration: N115ME
Serial No.: 51-11696

Span: 47.67 feet
Length: 34.25 feet
Height: 9.67 feet
Wing Area: 349 square feet
Empty Weight: 5890 pounds
Gross Weight: 7850 pounds
Max Speed: 215 mph
Service Ceiling: 20000 feet
Range: 700 miles
Location: Museum of Flight
Viewable

Iron Annie

Beech's twin-engine Model 18 helped the advance and growth of commercial aviation in the years before World War II. First flown in 1937, the Beech 18 was perfect for the private owner or charter operator. At the outbreak of World War II, versions of the plane were designated Model C-45 and used by the Army and Navy as trainers for pilots, gunners, bombardiers, and navigators as well as photographic reconnaissance planes and personnel transports. The last of more than seven thousand civilian and military versions of this series was built in 1969.

The First Lady of Aviation

Olive Ann Beech and her husband Walter established the Beech Aircraft Company in 1932. He was president and she was secretary-treasurer. During World War II, her husband was ill for a period of time and Mrs. Beech temporarily headed the company, helping prepare the military versions of the Beech 18. When Walter died in 1950, Olive Ann Beech was chairman of the board and president of the corporation. Under her leadership, Beech made aircraft, missile targets, aircraft components, and cryogenic fluid systems for the nation's space programs. Olive Ann Beech, named The First Lady of Aviation, was inducted into the National Aviation Hall of Fame in 1981.

Multi-engine Trainers

Most of the American pilots who flew the big bombers and cargo planes during World War II flew aircraft such as the Beech C-45s near the end of their training. After pilots had mastered the small single-engine trainers, the next step was bigger, two-engine craft. But pilots were not the only ones Beech planes helped train; around 90 percent of the nation's navigators and bombardiers as well as many aerial gunners learned their trade in Army and Navy versions of these Beech C-45s.

Flight Fact: Beech Model 18 aircraft were in continuous production for more than thirty years—longer than the famed DC-3!

de Havilland D.H. 106 Comet 4C

Manufacturer: de Havilland
Model: Comet 4C
Year: 1959
Registration: N888WA
Serial No.: 6424

Span: 114.83 feet
Length: 118 feet
Height: 28.5 feet
Wing Area: 2121 square feet
Gross Weight: 162000 pounds
Cruise Speed: 503 mph
Cruising Altitude: 39000 feet
Range: 2650 miles
Location: Restoration Center
(Everett, WA)
Viewable

An Aviation Marvel

First flown in 1949, the British-made Comet was the world's first jet airliner; it went into service on May 2, 1952. It was designed to give Great Britain a definite edge in post-World War II transport and it was an immediate success. Other commercial aircraft of the period such as the Douglas DC-6 could not compete with the technological and performance superiority of the Comet.

An Aviation Tragedy

However, just when it seemed the Comet had sewn up the commercial transport market, tragedy struck. Five deadly crashes, two within sixteen days of each other, revealed a design flaw that would eventually ground the original Comets for good. By the time the flaw had been corrected and the new Comet 4C had been produced, de Havilland's jet had lost its lead to the Boeing 707.

The Museum's Comet is believed to be the only one remaining in all of North America.

Boeing VC-137B Air Force One

Manufacturer: Boeing
Model: VC-137B
Year: 1958
Registration: None
Serial No.: 58-6970

Wing Span: 130.83 feet
Length: 144.5 feet
Height: 38.42 feet
Wing Area: 2433 square feet
Gross Weight: 258000 pounds
Max Speed: 590 mph
Service Ceiling: 40000 feet
Range: 4,000 mi
Location: Museum of Flight
Viewable

Air Force One—The Flying Oval Office

The first presidential jet plane, a specially-built Boeing 707-120, is known as SAM (Special Air Missions) 970. This aircraft, as well as any other Air Force aircraft, carried the call sign "Air Force One" when the president was aboard. Delivered in 1959 to replace Eisenhower's Super-Constellation, the high-speed jet transport is a flying Oval Office with a modified interior and sophisticated communication equipment.

Meeting the World Face-to-Face

Jet technology gives the United States president the opportunity to meet face-to-face with world leaders. SAM 970 carried presidents Eisenhower, Kennedy, Johnson, and Nixon, as well as VIPs, such as Nikita Khrushchev and Henry Kissinger.

By 1962, SAM 970 was replaced by a newer Boeing VC-137C. But SAM 970 remained in the presidential fleet, ferrying VIPs and the vice-president until June 1996.

The Museum's VC-137B is on loan from the U.S. Air Force Museum.

Boeing 727

A Boeing Classic

One of the world's classic airliners, the Boeing 727 was developed to provide economic low-altitude, high-speed cruising capability. The distinctive T-tail design allowed it to climb fast, and descend fast making it successful in smaller airports with short runways. An innovative auxiliary power unit (APU) eliminated the need for ground power or starting equipment in the more primitive airports of developing countries. It carried billions of passengers, in every corner of the world, on everything from short hops to cross-country flights.

Successful Marketing

To improve sales as it began rolling off the production line, Boeing flew a new 727 on a seventy-six thousand mile journey to introduce it to twenty-six countries. From the time it was first flown in February 1963, until production ended in 1984, a total of 1,832 Boeing 727s had rolled off factory lines and seen service with more than one hundred different airlines.

The Museum's airplane was the first 727 produced.

Manufacturer: Boeing
Model: 727-022
Year: 1962
Registration: N7001U
Serial No.: 18293

Span: 108 feet
Length: 133.17 feet
Height: 34 feet
Wing Area: 1650 square feet
Empty Weight: 80602 pounds
Gross Weight: 160000 pounds
Cruise Speed: 596 mph
Max Speed: 632 mph
Service Ceiling: 36100 feet
Range: 3430 miles
Location: Restoration Center
(Everett, WA)
Viewable

Boeing 737

Manufacturer: Boeing
Model: 737-130
Year: 1967
Registration: 515
Serial No.: 19437

Span: 93 feet
Length: 94 feet
Height: 37 feet
Wing Area: 980 square feet
Empty Weight: 56893 pounds
Gross Weight: 97800 pounds
Cruising Speed: 575 mph
Operating Ceiling: 35000 feet
Range: 2140 miles
Location: Storage
Not Viewable

The Prototype "Baby Boeing"

The 737 is the smallest and most popular jetliner in the Boeing airline family. Since 1967, over 3,000 Baby Boeings have been built or ordered. The 737 is dependable and versatile, which makes it popular with airlines throughout the world.

Praise from a NASA Pilot

"The 737 was a wonderful plane," says NASA research pilot Lee Person. "It could do things that other airplanes simply couldn't." High praise from the former Marine fighter pilot who's flown over 130 aircraft in his forty-one year career, including the Hawker XV-6A Kestrel (forerunner to the Harrier jet fighter). From 1974 to 1995, Person and fellow pilot Dick Yenni flew the 737 prototype in more than twenty different aerial research projects for NASA.

The Museum's aircraft is the first production 737. The prototype made its first flight with Brien Wygle and Lew Wallick at the controls on April 9, 1967. Boeing used the 737 as a flight test aircraft before it became NASA's Transport Systems Research Vehicle in 1974. Based at the Langley Research Center in Virginia, the 737 was used to test many technological innovations including a virtual cockpit, electronic flight displays and airborne wind shear detection systems.

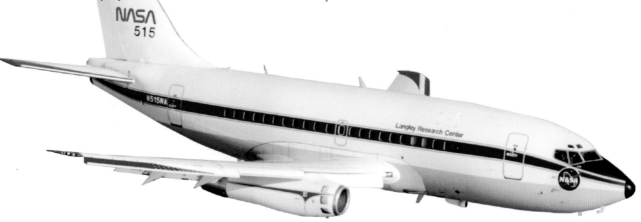

Boeing 747

Manufacturer: Boeing
Model: 747-121
Year: 1969
Registration: N747001
Serial No.: 20235

Span: 195.67 feet
Length: 231.33 feet
Height: 63.42 feet
Wing Area: 5500 square feet
Empty Weight: 348816 pounds
Gross Weight: 710000 pounds
Cruise Speed: 595 mph
Max Speed: 640 mph
Service Ceiling: 45000 feet
Range: 6000 miles
Location: Boeing Field
Viewable

Big Business—Big Risks

Merely recalling the early days of the 747 program "brings sweat to the palms of my hands," Boeing's then-president, William Allen, said years after the giant aircraft had been developed. Requiring the company to risk much of its net worth, the development of the world's largest passenger aircraft was a formidable undertaking. With seating for 374 passengers (up to 550 in some configurations), a weight at takeoff of more than 300 tons, and enough fuel in its tanks to power a small automobile around the globe thirty-six times, the 747 astounded the world and is easily recognized as a milestone in the evolution of aviation design.

The Museum's 747 is the prototype. It was used by The Boeing Company for myriad flight test programs over the course of many years. Almost twenty-six years after its roll-out, this 747 served as a flying test-bed for the state-of-the-art Boeing 777 engine program. With a tail that is some six-stories tall, it is too large to fit inside the Museum's Great Gallery, but can be viewed on Boeing Field just north of the Museum.

Military Aircraft

The ordinary air fighter is an extraordinary man and the extraordinary air fighter stands as one in a million among his fellows.

–Theodore Roosevelt

Robert Kelly

I don't remember even seeing an aircraft before that day at age five when I was taken for a flight out of Butte, Montana. I was enthralled with everything, especially the aircraft itself, rolling down the runway—Fast! Levitating! Climbing higher and higher, until there were toy cars in the tiny streets with their tiny buildings below us! I knew I had to be a pilot. The flight was a present after having spent several weeks in the hospital, where I was deeply impressed with the surgeon and nurses and had made the firm decision to be a doctor!

In subsequent years, I was able to maintain both ambitions and, thanks to the U.S. Navy and luck, I became a Naval Aviator, flying from aircraft carriers before going to medical school and flight surgeon training, thus becoming a Naval Aviator/Flight Surgeon. In this capacity my assignments involved piloting single and multiengine prop and jet aircraft in operations off of several aircraft carriers. When I graduated from Navy Test Pilot School, I began to combine my doctoring skills with some **real** flying. While at the Navy Test Center I evaluated problems in new aircraft or new aircraft systems in the areas of man-machine relationships, controls and displays, escape systems, and environmental control systems. There were many aircraft to be flown—from props to jets to helicopters—and lots of test projects to complete.

My favorite jet has always been the F-8 Crusader; what a great feeling to see such an exotic flying machine waiting for you. Rigged out in all your flight gear, you walk out to inspect and lay hands on that beautiful product of aviation technology, climb aboard, get strapped in and suddenly you know you are in command. It is impossible to not get excited by the thrust of jet engines, the rapid escape from earth and the smoothness of flight. Imagine taking a 60-foot, multimillion dollar piece of equipment into the air. Imagine landing on an aircraft carrier on a pitch black night in a storm. Imagine being hundreds of miles from shore and low on fuel. I remember getting out of the aircraft after many such flights and becoming aware that my flight suit was soaked with sweat. The total mental involvement with the carrier approach, and the elation with the accomplishment, allows no other distraction. Where else in the world could all this have happened for a small boy but through the United States Military? And they paid us to do it!

One hundred years ago nearly everyone knew that man could never fly. Now, it's part of everyday life. Military aviation—like all manned, powered, controllable flight—started with the Wright brothers. The first U.S.Army aircraft in 1908 looked like the Wright Flyer. Just a few generations later, my first assignment as an Aviator/Flight Surgeon placed me in a fighter operational test squadron (VX-4) where I flew a variety of aircraft, including the F-8, F-4, A-4 and S-2. One generation later, my sons were flying F-14s, F/A-18s, P-3s, C-130s, 727s and DC-9s—either entirely new aircraft with much more complex systems, or existing aircraft with improved systems yielding more effective performance. That sort of huge surge in new types of aircraft with enormous increases in sophistication continues to the present day—a great bounty of magnificent aircraft.

—*Robert Kelly* M.D., Test Pilot and Flight Surgeon, U.S. Navy

Curtiss JN-4D Jenny

Such Popularity

The JN-4 was the only American aircraft to have played a major role in World War I. Over 90 percent of North American combat pilots learned to fly in the Jenny. After the war, the surplus aircraft, many still in cartons, were sold off, some for as little as a couple hundred dollars. Most became the aircraft of choice for the new breed of pilot known as barnstormers. Other purchasers of these "planes in a box" included Charles Lindbergh and Amelia Earhart.

See-Through View

The Museum's Jenny is restored to flyable condition, but the fabric has not been applied because of the public interest in viewing the intricate wood construction of the wings and fuselage.

The Museum's Jenny took over 9,500 hours of highly skilled craftsmanship to restore. Nearly all of the metal fittings are original Jenny parts but only the upper wing spars remained of the original 1917 wooden components. The Curtiss 90 horsepower OX-5 engine has also been restored to original 1917 configuration.

Restoration work was accomplished by the crew of the Lucy T. Whittier Screen Door and Flying Machine Company in Friday Harbor, Washington. The Curtiss OX-5 engine was donated in memory of Arnold T. Cassidy.

Manufacturer: Curtiss
Model: JN-4D Jenny
Year: 1917
Registration: None
Serial No.: None

Span: 43.61 feet
Length: 27.33 feet
Height: 9.89 feet
Wing Area: 352 square feet
Empty Weight: 1390 pounds
Gross Weight: 1920 pounds
Cruise Speed: 60 mph
Max Speed: 75 mph
Service Ceiling: 6500 feet
Location: Museum of Flight
Viewable

Manufacturer: Caproni
Model: Ca 20
Year: 1914
Registration: None
Serial No.: 1

Span: 26 feet
Length: 27.43 feet
Height: 9.5 feet
Wing Area: 144 square feet
Empty Weight: 778 pounds
Max Speed: 103 mph
Location: Museum of Flight
Viewable

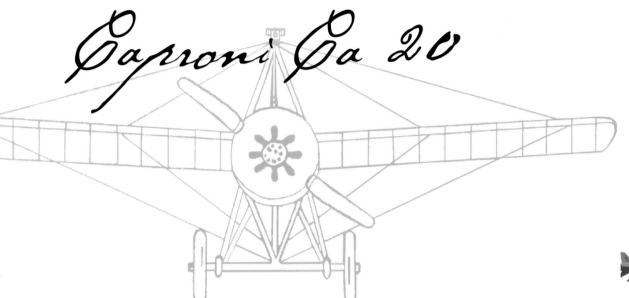

Caproni Ca 20

Caproni Ca 20 (continued)

The World's First Fighter Plane

The Caproni Ca 20 was an aircraft ahead of its time in design, purpose, and armament. In early 1914, before World War I, this speedy single-seat monoplane was built with a forward-facing machine gun mounted above the propeller arc. Considered the world's first fighter plane, the Ca 20's pilot could aim the overhead machine gun at enemy aircraft via a false sight at eye level.

Speedy Monoplane in a Biplane World

Built as a derivative of the Caproni's Ca 18 reconnaissance airplane, the Ca 20 incorporated a larger engine covered by a streamlined cowling, shorter wings, and a machine gun as an offensive weapon.

Gianni Caproni (1886-1957): The Count Who Built Planes

Gianni Caproni designed his first airplane, the Ca 1, in 1910—only seven years after the Wright brothers' famous flight. During World War I, his company created a famous line of heavy bombers, including the Caproni Ca 3, versions of which were produced in the United States, England, and France, as well as in Italy. After the war, the growing Caproni Aircraft Company switched from bombers to civilian passenger and transport aircraft.

Between airplane designs, Gianni Caproni devised and patented many components, including armored and variable-pitch airscrews (propellers), an anemometer (wind gauge), an engine compressor, steerable undercarriages, and a machine gun driven by centrifugal force. Caproni was awarded the title Count of Taliedo by the King of Italy in 1940 and remained active in his company until his death in 1957.

Never Restored—and It Shows

The Caproni Ca 20 may not be as crisp, clean, and pretty as the day it was rolled from the workshop, but that's part of its beauty. Unlike most aircraft in museum collections, this plane is almost entirely original. It wears the skin applied in 1914, and today that battered skin can be seen with all of the scars and stains of almost a century of life.

Flight Fact: The Ca 20 was an exceptional airplane, but the Italian military wanted the Caproni Company to focus on heavy bombers. The Museum's Ca 20 is the only one ever produced. The plane was stored by the Caproni family in Italy for over eighty-five years before being acquired by the Museum of Flight in 1999.

Albatros D.Va

Manufacturer: Albatros
Model: D.Va
Year: 1917
Registration: NX36DV
Serial No.: Reproduction

Span: 26.69 feet
Length: 24.06 feet
Height: 8.85 feet
Wing Area: 229 square feet
Empty Weight: 1511 pounds
Gross Weight: 2061 pounds
Max Speed: 103 mph
Max. Altitude: 20500 feet
Max. Range: 2 hours
Location: Champlin Fighter Museum
(Mesa, AZ)
Viewable

Of All the Fighting Planes . . .

The Albatros D.Va first entered service during May of 1917 and remained a primary combatant until the end of World War I. It was numerically one of the most significant German fighters during the 1917 through 1918 period.

An Exercise in Accuracy

This aircraft in the Champlin Collection is an extremely accurate full-scale reproduction that was built in two stages. The airframe and wings were manufactured in Germany by Art Williams. Final assembly and finish-out later were undertaken by Jim and Zona Appleby, then of Riverside, California. Both parties have extraordinary reputations for the quality of their work, and this aircraft fully exemplifies that. Underscoring its builders' penchant for accuracy, this Albatros is equipped with a rare, original Mercedes D.IIIa six-cylinder water-cooled engine. The very colorful markings of the Museum's Champlin Collection replica Albatros D.Va is painted in the markings of "JagGeschwader 2" representing those of German ace George van Hippe. When completed the Albatros D.Va was delivered by ground transport to the Champlin Museum in 1984.

Aviatik D.1

Manufacturer: Aviatik
Model: D.I (Berg Scout)
Year: 1918
Registration: None
Serial No.: 101.4

Span: 26.25 feet
Length: 22.98 feet
Height: 9.19 feet
Wing Area: 221.4 square feet
Empty Weight: 1540 pounds
Gross Weight: 1870 pounds
Max Speed: 116.6 mph at 3,280 feet
Max. Range: 1.5 hours
Location: Champlin Fighter Museum
(Mesa, AZ)
Viewable

A Special Purchase

The Champlin Collection's Aviatik was purchased in Europe by Art Williams. Following considerable research, Williams discovered he had acquired an extremely rare aircraft built by Thone and Fiala. Perhaps as important was the fact this particular Aviatik actually was owned and operated by the Berg aircraft company and at one time had been part of the Berg estate. During the restoration that followed, attention was paid to recreating as accurately as possible, the original, highly unusual color scheme used during the Aviatik's military career. It eventually was painted in markings generically representing noted Austro-Hungarian aces Frank Linke-Crawford (twenty-seven victories), Julius Arigi (thirty-two victories), and Bela Macourek (five victories).

Champlin acquired the aircraft in 1978 and completed it in Arizona. Among the unique aspects of the restoration was the decision to build, from scratch, a totally new brass radiator for the exceptionally rare Austro-Daimler engine. Additionally, a pair of extremely rare Schwarzlose machine guns were provided to complete a truly remarkable restoration.

A Rare One

The Museum's Champlin Collection original Aviatik D.I is an extremely rare original example of the first indigenous Austro-Hungarian single-seat fighter to enter production. There is only one other example known to exist.

Fokker Dr.1 Triplane

Manufacturer: Fokker
Model: Dr.I
Year: 1917
Registration: NX2203
Serial No.: Reproduction

Span: 23.62 feet
Length: 18.93 feet
Height: 7.88 feet
Wing Area: 201.5 square feet
Empty Weight: 893.2 pounds
Gross Weight: 1289.2 pounds
Max Speed: 103.12 mph
Max. Altitude: 19600 feet
Max. Range: 1.5 hours
Location: Champlin Fighter Museum
(Mesa, AZ)
Viewable

Famous Plane—Famous Pilots

The Dr.I, Dreidecker, often referred to informally as the Fokker Triplane, was one of the most famous German combat aircraft of World War I. It was flown by many competent and well-known German pilots; the most famous was the legendary Manfred von Richthofen, who first flew a Dreidecker during September 1917. He remained a strong proponent of the aircraft until his death on April 21, 1918, in Dr.I #425/17.

Flight Fact: There are no known surviving original Fokker Dr.Is. The last original aircraft was destroyed during an Allied bombing raid on Berlin during World War II.

Dentist Richard Coughlin of New York began construction on the Champlin Collection's replica during 1958, completing it in 1972. When the Dr.I was seriously damaged in an accident, Doug Champlin acquired the wreckage and, in 1978, had it completely rebuilt. During 1990, the Warner Scarab radial engine that had been used by Coughlin was replaced with an authentic Le Rhone rotary.

Fokker D.VII

A Confidence Builder

Historically, the Fokker D.VII is considered by most authorities to be the most significant combat aircraft of World War I. Created by the great Fokker engineering genius Reinhold Platz, the D.VII was the scourge of the skies over Europe during the last year of the war. Pilots found the D.VII was easy to fly and generated confidence, with specific control attributes that permitted distinct advantages when engaged in air-to-air combat. For example, stalls were predictable and controllable.

The Museum's Champlin Collection Fokker D.VII replica is an extremely accurate rendering of the original aircraft including the engine. This reproduction aircraft was started by noted aircraft replica builder, Joe DeFiori. After buying the basic steel-tube fuselage from Joe, Doug Champlin shipped it to Jim and Zona Appleby who completed the aircraft for Museum display. Equipped with an original Mercedes water-cooled, six-cylinder engine, it was authentically painted in the unique lozenge-pattern camouflage of the period and given the attractive winged sword emblem of Germany's forty-victory ace, Rudolf Berthold.

Manufacturer: Fokker
Model: D.VII
Year: 1918
Registration: N38038
Serial No.: Reproduction

Span: 29.29 feet
Length: 24.06 feet
Height: 8.85 feet
Wing Area: 229 square feet
Empty Weight: 1511 pounds
Gross Weight: 2061 pounds
Max Speed: 103 mph
Max. Altitude: 20500 feet
Max. Range: 2 hours
Location: Champlin Fighter Museum
(Mesa, AZ)
Viewable

Fokker D.VIII

Manufacturer: Fokker
Model: D.VIII
Year: 1918
Registration: NX7557U
Serial No.: Reproduction

Span: 27.37 feet
Length: 19.23 feet
Height: 8.53 feet
Wing Area: 115.5 square feet
Empty Weight: 893 pounds
Gross Weight: 1334 pounds
Max Speed: 103127.5 mph
Max. Altitude: 19680 feet
Max. Range: 1.5 hours
Location: Champlin Fighter Museum
(Mesa, AZ)
Viewable

Fame Found It Late

The Fokker D.VIII's unusual parasol monoplane configuration was perhaps the most advanced aircraft of World War I. Designed by Fokker's engineering genius, Reinhold Platz, the D.VIII was a highly maneuverable aircraft that would have been a formidable opponent if it had not been so late in entering the war.

Flight Fact: Today, only a single authentic D.VIII exists, located in the Museo Dell'Aeronautica Gianni Caproni in Trento, Italy.

The Champlin Collection's replica aircraft was built during the 1960s by E. O. Swearingen of Worth, Illinois. Swearingen reviewed the surviving aircraft in Italy and later corresponded with Platz in order to authenticate the accuracy of his work. Following the aircraft's completion by Swearingen, it was flown for sport.

In 1980, Doug Champlin purchased the aircraft. It is still equipped with the Warner radial that Swearingen used. The Museum's Champlin Collection replica Fokker D.VIII carries an authentic camouflage scheme and is powered by a conventional radial rather than an actual rotary engine. Future plans involve re-equipping the D.VIII with an authentic Oberursel rotary engine.

Fokker E.111

Manufacturer: Fokker
Model: E.III
Year: 1915
Registration: N3363G
Serial No.: Reproduction

Span: 31.23 feet
Length: 23.54 feet
Height: 7.88 feet
Wing Area: 172.8 square feet
Empty Weight: 878 pounds
Gross Weight: 1342 pounds
Max Speed: 87.5 mph
Max. Altitude: 12000 feet
Max. Range: 1.5 hours
Location: Champlin Fighter Museum
(Mesa, AZ)
Viewable

New Technology Makes its Mark

The E.III, sometimes referred to as the "Eindecker" (meaning "one wing"), deserves a significant place in aviation history not necessarily because of its aerial prowess, but because it was the first combat aircraft in the world to be equipped with a forward-firing, fixed machine gun synchronized to fire between the propeller blades.

The E.III was the third and most important permutation of the original monoplane Fokker family. Being a small but important step forward in the evolution of the fighter, it is important to note this aircraft used wing warping for roll control, rather than the "more advanced" aileron flight control system.

Flight Fact: The Museum's Champlin Collection E.III is considered one of the most authentic replicas of this aircraft in the world as it emulates the original in every respect.

The Champlin Collection's replica aircraft was commissioned by Doug Champlin and built during 1981 by Jim and Zona Appleby, of Riverside, California. Typical of an Appleby reproduction, it is extremely accurate in detail. It is equipped with an authentic World War I vintage Oberursel rotary engine and an authentic Spandau machine gun offset to the starboard side of the forward engine cowling.

Nieuport Type 27

The French Perspective

Developed from the earlier successful Nieuport 11, Nieuport 17, and Nieuport 24 pursuit aircraft, the Nieuport 27 was an agile and well-armed adversary that was very much a match for most German pursuit aircraft of the last two years of World War I. Many of France's most accomplished pilots flew the Nieuport 27 in combat. With it, they generated a very high kill/loss ratio. Pilots found the Nieuport 27 to have few vices and many attributes.

The Champlin Collection aircraft is a full-scale reproduction of this important French combat aircraft of World War I, created by master builders Carl Swanson and Jerry Thornhill in 1980. In consideration of strength and safety issues, this replica was built with a steel tube structure rather than wood. Also, brakes and a small tailwheel were added. Regardless of these slight deviations, the aircraft is visually almost an exact replica of the original aircraft. The authentic look is underscored by a vintage Gnome-Rhone rotary engine.

Doug Champlin acquired the aircraft shortly after it was completed in 1980. The Museum's Champlin Collection Nieuport 27 replica is equipped with a single over-wing Lewis machine gun and is painted in British markings.

Manufacturer: Nieuport
Model: 27
Year: 1917
Registration: N5597M
Serial No.: Reproduction

Span: 26.83 feet
Length: 19.29 feet
Height: 7.96 feet
Wing Area: 158.77 square feet
Empty Weight: 782 pounds
Gross Weight: 1540 pounds
Max Speed: 128 mph
Max. Altitude: 18200 feet
Max. Range: 2 hours
Location: Champlin Fighter Museum
(Mesa, AZ)
Viewable

Nieuport Type 28

Made in France, but Used by Americans

This aircraft is a rare original example of one of the least-heralded, but aesthetically most attractive, of all World War I fighters. It represents the last of the Nieuport biplanes to enter combat during WW I—though it did so under the auspices of the American Expeditionary Forces only. Surprisingly, it was not adopted for service by the French Aviation Militaire. Beginning in March 1918, U.S. forces eventually received 297 of these aircraft.

We Have a Problem

Not well liked by pilots due to a tendency to shed wing fabric during high-speed dives, the Nieuport 28 was pulled from operational service only four months after its combat debut.

The Champlin Collection's aircraft was restored during 1998 and 1999 by noted World War I aircraft rebuilder Roger Freeman of Marlin, Texas. It was delivered to the Champlin Museum in April 1999 and is seen in authentic American Expeditionary Forces markings.

Manufacturer: Nieuport
Model: 28
Year: 1918
Registration: None
Serial No.: 14

Span: 26.77 feet
Length: 21 feet
Height: 8.21 feet
Wing Area: 172.23 square feet
Empty Weight: 961 pounds
Gross Weight: 1539 pounds
Max Speed: 123 mph
Max. Altitude: 18500 feet
Max. Range: 2 hours
Location: Champlin Fighter Museum
(Mesa, AZ)
Viewable

Pfalz D.XII

Manufacturer: Pfalz
Model: D.XII
Year: 1918
Registration: N43C
Serial No.: 3498

Span: 29.53 feet
Length: 20.83 feet
Height: 8.85 feet
Wing Area: 126.2 square feet
Empty Weight: 1571 pounds
Gross Weight: 1539 pounds
Max Speed: 106.25 mph
Max. Altitude: 18500 feet
Max. Range: 2.5 hours
Location: Champlin Fighter Museum
(Mesa, AZ)
Viewable

In the Right Hands

This aircraft is a rare original example of one of the most competitive, yet least-heralded German fighter aircraft of World War I. Overshadowed by the Fokker D.VII, it was nevertheless every bit the D.VII's equal—and in some respects, it was superior. It was a fierce combatant in the hands of a competent pilot.

The Champlin Collection aircraft is an immaculately restored authentic World War I survivor. Following combat, it was captured by U.S. forces and in late 1918, was one of two Pfalz D.XIIs brought to the U.S. for examination. Winding up in civilian hands, it was used in the noteworthy movie *Dawn Patrol*, among others, and from there was sold to Colonel G. B. Jarrett to become part of his famous collection in Atlantic City, New Jersey. Hollywood pilot Frank Tallman acquired this Pfalz in 1958 for his collection, and it was restored by Robert Rust of Atlanta, Georgia. When the Tallman collection was auctioned off in 1968, the aircraft was acquired by Dolph Overton's Wings and Wheels collection of Orlando, Florida. Champlin acquired it during another auction in 1981.

Rumpler Taube

Manufacturer: Rumpler
Model: Taube
Year: 1910
Registration: None
Serial No.: Reproduction

Span: 45.83 feet
Length: 33.5 feet
Height: 10.5 feet
Wing Area: 280 square feet
Empty Weight: 950 pounds
Gross Weight: 1200 pounds
Max Speed: 60 mph
Max. Altitude: 10000 feet
Max. Range: 4 hours
Location: Champlin Fighter Museum
(Mesa, AZ)
Viewable

The Dove

The Rumpler Taube was one of the last of the pre-World War I, first-generation aircraft to be utilized in combat. Seriously outdated by the outbreak of World War I in 1914, the Rumpler Taube was nevertheless built in significant quantities by a large number and variety of manufacturers. By 1915, its shortcomings—including a maximum speed of only 60 mph—were readily apparent to all who flew or serviced it. As a result, it quickly became one of the most vulnerable of all combat aircraft types utilized during the first months of the war. The Taube soon was removed from front line service as an observation platform and quickly relegated to less demanding roles such as training.

Flight Fact: The Taube still used wing-warping for roll control during a period when virtually everything in the skies was equipped with ailerons.

Master craftsman Art Williams undertook construction of the Champlin Collection replica in 1961. It was completed in 1984 and delivered to Doug Champlin shortly thereafter. It is a near exact replica including an original Mercedes D.IIIa engine, an extremely rare 120 hp version, which was restored by Jim Appleby of California and Art Williams in Germany.

RAF S.E.5a

Manufacturer: Royal Aircraft Factory
Model: S.E.5a
Year: 1917
Registration: NX910AV
Serial No.: Reproduction

Span: 26.62 feet
Length: 20.92 feet
Height: 9.5 feet
Wing Area: 245.8 square feet
Empty Weight: 1531 pounds
Gross Weight: 2048 pounds
Max Speed: 126 mph at 10,000 feet
Max. Altitude: 17000 feet
Max. Range: 2.5 hours
Location: Champlin Fighter Museum
(Mesa, AZ)
Viewable

A Very Capable Plane

The S.E.5a was one of the most important British combat aircraft of World War I. Some of the greatest of all Allied aces utilized the S.E.5a in combat including Major Edward Mannock with seventy-three total victories (fifty in the S.E.5a), Lieutenant Colonel Billy Bishop, and Captain James McCudden. These and many other pilots considered the S.E.5a's extraordinary strength and stability to be its most significant attributes, though it was equally capable in terms of speed and maneuverability.

The Museum's Champlin Collection S.E.5a is a perfect replica of the original, delivered to Champlin in 1988 and completed and placed on display during 1989. It was one of three S.E.5a reproductions begun by Bobby Strahlmann, Tom Davis, and Gil Bodine in Florida during 1971. Inside and out, it duplicates the details of the original aircraft and is painted in the markings of American World War I ace George A. Vaughn who served with No. 84 Squadron, Royal Flying Corps. The markings depict his aircraft on August 22, 1918, the day he scored his fifth aerial victory.

Sopwith Triplane

Manufacturer: Sopwith
Model: Triplane
Year: 1916
Registration: N38057
Serial No.: Reproduction

Span: 26.5 feet
Length: 18.83 feet
Height: 10.5 feet
Wing Area: 231 square feet
Empty Weight: 1101 pounds
Gross Weight: 1541 pounds
Max Speed: 117 mph
Max. Altitude: 20500 feet
Max. Range: 2 hours
Location: Champlin Fighter Museum
(Mesa, AZ)
Viewable

Bring on the Competition

The precedent-setting Sopwith Triplane, when it first appeared over the front during late 1916, was the most maneuverable production fighter in the world. Its affect on other countries' pursuit designs, particularly Germany's, was profound. Within months of its unveiling, virtually every German pursuit manufacturer had a triplane either under development or in production.

The Sopwith Triplane served in both the Royal Flying Corps and the Royal Naval Air Service. The latter was the most important user. Though the Triplane's air combat successes were many and seemingly unending, by August 1917 it was being rapidly phased out of service and replaced by the more capable Sopwith Camel.

Normal Triplane armament consisted of a single fixed Vickers machine gun mounted in the center of the upper fuselage ahead of the cockpit and synchronized to fire through the propeller disk.

The Champlin Collection's Sopwith Triplane, built by Carl Swanson of Darien, Wisconsin, is virtually an exact reproduction of the original aircraft with an original Clerget rotary engine and original gun and instruments. It is authentically painted in the markings of Canadian ace, Sub-Lieutenant Mel Alexander's aircraft, *Black Prince*.

Sopwith Pup

Manufacturer: Sopwith
Model: Pup
Year: 1916
Registration: NX6018
Serial No.: Reproduction

Span: 26.5 feet
Length: 19.31 feet
Height: 9.42 feet
Wing Area: 254 square feet
Empty Weight: 787 pounds
Gross Weight: 1225 pounds
Max Speed: 111.5 mph
Max. Altitude: 18500 feet
Max. Range: 1.75 hours
Location: Champlin Fighter Museum
(Mesa, AZ)
Viewable

The Perfect Pup

The Sopwith Pup ranks as one of the truly great combat aircraft of World War I. Some have called it the most perfect flying machine ever made. Regardless, the Pup was undeniably a docile and enjoyable airplane to fly. A true pursuit, the Pup was capable of competing one-on-one with any air combat aircraft in the sky at the time of its debut during the spring of 1916. It proved so effective against German aircraft that German pilots consciously avoided confrontations with it until the advent of more capable German pursuits. By the end of 1917, the Pup's advantage had been offset by newer designs. It was quickly phased-out as more advanced aircraft became available.

The Pup was equipped with a single-fixed, synchronized Vickers machine gun mounted on top of the forward fuselage, ahead of the cockpit.

The Champlin Collection's Pup, which was acquired from Jim Ricklef of California, is an exact reproduction of the original aircraft. It was built by Carl Swanson of Darien, Wisconsin and is considered a masterpiece of replication. It is virtually indistinguishable from an original aircraft—right down to the Le Rhone rotary engine.

Sopwith Camel

World War I Fame

Developed from the successful Sopwith Pup, the Sopwith Camel is considered by many to be the single most famous aircraft type of World War I. Flown by various Allied combatants throughout the last two years of the war, the Camel was the favored mount of some of the war's most famous aces. Camels destroyed no less than 1,294 enemy aircraft—a kill total greater than that of any other single aircraft type of the war. Worth noting is the fact that a Camel is claimed by some historians to have been the downfall of Germany's most famous World War I ace, Manfred von Richthofen.

In the right hands, the Camel was an effective weapon. It was highly maneuverable, well armed, and quick enough to work one-on-one with any enemy aircraft. Only the German Fokker Dr.I triplane was an even match in terms of maneuverability.

Flight Fact: The name "Camel" was derived from the hump-shaped cover over the machine guns. The Champlin Collection's Camel reproduction was acquired from Jim and Zona Appleby's Antique Aero Limited of Riverside, California during 1979. The Appleby replica is highly authentic, differing from the original aircraft in detail only: It has a radial instead of rotary engine, main gear brakes, improved instrumentation, and a tail wheel.

Manufacturer: Sopwith
Model: F.1 Camel
Year: 1917
Registration: NX6330
Serial No.: Reproduction

Span: 28 feet
Length: 18.75 feet
Height: 8.5 feet
Wing Area: 231 square feet
Empty Weight: 962 pounds
Gross Weight: 1482 pounds
Max Speed: 104.5 mph at 10, 000 feet
Max. Altitude: 18000 feet
Max. Range: 2.5 hours
Location: Champlin Fighter Museum
(Mesa, AZ)
Viewable

Sopwith Snipe

Manufacturer: Sopwith
Model: 7F.1 Snipe
Year: 1918
Registration: NX6765D
Serial No.: Reproduction

Span: 31.08 feet
Length: 19.83 feet
Height: 8.25 feet
Wing Area: 271 square feet
Empty Weight: 1312 pounds
Gross Weight: 2020 pounds
Max Speed: 121 mph at 10, 000 feet
Max. Altitude: 10000 feet
Max. Range: 3 hours
Location: Champlin Fighter Museum
(Mesa, AZ)
Viewable

Improved Big Brother

The unqualified successes of the Sopwith Camel, coupled with the development of a new and powerful rotary engine—the B. R. 2—led to the birth of a new Sopwith pursuit designated the 7F.1 and named Snipe. The Snipe first flew in late 1917 and by the spring of 1918, orders for over 1,800 aircraft had been received. The first production Snipe followed during the summer.

Initial combat sorties indicated it was at least as good as the Camel in all important aspects, and in fact could outclimb it to any altitude. Most importantly, it was a better handling aircraft, which pleased pilots immensely. Very few Snipes actually saw combat due to the type's late arrival in the war. But even with its limited experience, those who flew it concluded it probably was the best British pursuit of World War I.

The Snipe was equipped with two Vickers machine guns mounted above and behind the engine and synchronized to fire forward through the propeller disk.

The Champlin Collection's Snipe was built by replica and antique builder Richard Day of Colonia, New Jersey. Completed in 1982, it is an authentic, full-scale reproduction of the postwar Snipe painted in typical post-World War I Royal Air Force markings. It differs from the original primarily in having a 220 horsepower Continental radial engine rather than a rotary.

SPAD XIII

Manufacturer: SPAD
Model: XIII
Year: 1917
Registration: NX3883F
Serial No.: Reproduction

Span: 26.31 feet
Length: 20.33 feet
Height: 7.54 feet
Wing Area: 227 square feet
Empty Weight: 1245 pounds
Gross Weight: 1807 pounds
Max Speed: 138 mph
Max. Altitude: 21820 feet
Max. Range: 2 hours
Location: Champlin Fighter Museum
(Mesa, AZ)
Viewable

Popularity Reigns

The SPAD XIII began replacing its predecessor, the SPAD VII, in frontline service during the summer and fall of 1917. Not surprisingly, it was a superb air combat platform and well liked by its pilots. It quickly became the standard French pursuit and concurrently, became quite popular with U.S. pilots of the American Expeditionary Forces. The most famous U.S. pilot of the war, Capt. Edward Rickenbacker, much preferred the SPAD XIII over other available pursuits and used one for most of his twenty-six aerial victories.

The SPAD XIII armament package usually consisted of two synchronized Vickers machine guns mounted just ahead of the cockpit and firing forward through the propeller disk.

The Champlin Collection's replica aircraft was built by Richard Day of Colonia, New Jersey. Because the original SPAD XIII drawings were destroyed during World War II, Day resorted to measurements taken from original SPADs owned by the National Air & Space Museum and the Cole Palen collection. Master builder Herb Tischler eventually helped finish the aircraft by completing the metal work and other miscellaneous requirements. Final assembly, with the original Hispano-Suiza engine, guns and instruments was undertaken at the Champlin Museum. The Champlin aircraft is painted in the markings of noted U.S. World War I ace, the Arizona Balloon Buster, Lt. Frank Luke.

Nieuport Type 24

A "New" Nieuport

The Nieuport 24 was the immediate successor to the Nieuport 17 but incorporated a number of changes. The Nieuport 24 was better streamlined with rounded, instead of flat sides, provided by means of horizontal stringers. The tail had a curved leading edge, a small fin and rounded horn-balanced rudder. This aircraft was used in limited numbers with the French Flying Service but the Americans purchased 287 machines for use at their training schools in France.

The Museum's Nieuport 24 is a reproduction, which was started by Walt Redfern and Skeeter Carlson of Spokane. Later the project was obtained by the late Johnnie Hart of Vancouver, Washington. Ron Ochs acquired the project in 1992, finished it according to Redfern plans, and donated it to the Museum. It is fitted with an 80hp LeRhone rotary engine that was originally in a WWI Tommy Morse Scout. The aircraft first flew in October 1995.

Manufacturer: Nieuport
Model: 24
Year: 1916
Registration: N24RL
Serial No.: Reproduction

Span: 26.92 feet
Length: 19 feet
Height: 7.96 feet
Wing Area: 158.77 square feet
Empty Weight: 782 pounds
Gross Weight: 1207 pounds
Max Speed: 110 mph
Max. Altitude: 17700 feet
Max. Range: 155 miles
Location: Storage, Oregon
Not Viewable

Boeing 100//P-12

Manufacturer: Boeing
Model: 100
Year: 1928
Registration: N872H
Serial No.: 1143

Span: 30 feet
Length: 20.58 feet
Height: 9.58 feet
Wing Area: 227.5 square feet
Empty Weight: 1665 pounds
Gross Weight: 2557 pounds
Cruise Speed: 142 mph
Max Speed: Speed 169 mph
Range: 520 miles
Location: Museum of Flight
Viewable

Famous Fighter Family

In 1928, Boeing developed the first in a family of fighters that would be one of their most successful designs between wars. The Model 83 was a biplane fighter that flew at nearly 170 mph (272 kph)—considered hot-rod performance for its day. Refined and improved versions became the Army P-12, the Navy F4B, and the Model 100 series. Nearly six hundred examples of Boeing's "Fighter Family" were built.

Changes in Design

The P-12/F4B fighter series, developed between world wars, is a mixture of old and new design components. Although many civil aircraft were built as monoplanes in the late-1920s, the military still wanted proven, World War I-style biplanes. While the Boeing fighters were still primarily cloth-covered, they incorporated corrugated aluminum control and tail surfaces. The wing structure was made of wood, but the fuselage was aluminum tubing. The P-12/F4B series was Boeing's last biplane fighter

Flight Fact: In 1936, the Museum's aircraft, then owned by Milo Burcham, flew from Los Angeles to San Diego upside down!

The Museum's Boeing Model 100 was one of four built as commercial/export versions of the Navy F4B-1. This one was sold to Pratt & Whitney and was used as a flying test bed for engines. It was then sold to stunt and air show pilot Milo Burcham. Purchased by movie pilot Paul Mantz in 1948, it appears in the background of many aviation films. In 1977 the fighter was restored to flyable condition and given an Army P-12 paint job.

Stearman PT-13A Kaydet

Famous American Trainer

The Stearman Kaydet, originally designed for civilian aviation, was adopted by the U.S. Army and Navy as a primary trainer from 1936 to 1945. Known as Stearmans, they were actually built by Boeing who, in 1934, had acquired the Stearman Aircraft Company. The design was practically considered an antique when introduced, but the biplanes were rugged, maneuverable, and ideal for the rigors of military flight training. Most Stearmans survived the war and many became prized as crop dusters and air show performers.

Classrooms in the Sky

A generation of young American military aviators started their flight training in Kaydets before flying the powerful fighters, bombers, and transports of World War II. Navy men nicknamed these trainers "Yellow Perils," both because of their all-yellow paint schemes and the danger of flying near swarms of inexperienced student pilots in the little biplanes. Most American pilots from the World War II era took their first solo flights in versions of Stearman's forgiving Kaydet. A student graduated from primary flight training with about sixty-five hours of flight time amassed over about nine weeks of training.

Flight Fact: While over 8,585 of the Boeing-Stearman biplanes were built, the manufacture of spare components and replacement parts make the total production run equivalent to 10,346 planes.

Manufacturer: Stearman
Model: PT-13A Kaydet
Year: 1937
Registration: N8FL
Serial No.: 75-055

Span: 32.17 feet
Length: 24.02 feet
Height: 9.17 feet
Wing Area: 297.4 square feet
Empty Weight: 1936 pounds
Gross Weight: 2717 pounds
Cruise Speed: 106 mph
Max Speed: 124 mph
Service Ceiling: 11200 feet
Range: 505 miles
Location: Museum of Flight
Viewable

The Museum's Kaydet, manufactured as an Army PT-13A, was modified to a PT-13C during World War II, but was restored with a Continental R-670 engine of the PT-17 model. Built in 1937, it was the fifty-fifth of over 8,585 Kaydets produced. It was donated to the Museum in 1983 by William I. Phillips and has been flown at Museum-sponsored special events.

Lockheed P-38 L Lightning

Manufacturer: Lockheed
Model: P-38L/M Lightning
Year: 1944
Registration: NL3JB
Serial No.: 44-53097

Span: 52 feet
Length: 37 feet
Height: 9.83 feet
Wing Area: 327.5 square feet
Empty Weight: 12780 pounds
Gross Weight: 21600 pounds
Max Speed: 414 mph at 25000 feet
Max. Altitude: 44000 feet
Max. Range: 1175 miles
Location: Champlin Fighter Museum
(Mesa, AZ)
Viewable

Ocean Flier

The most distinguishing feature of the P-38 was its podded fuselage and unusual twin-boom tail assembly. Initially an innovative approach to meet a 1937 Air Corps specification, it would later prove ideal for the Pacific Theatre and the long, over-water flights that often were entailed.

Variations in Design

Perhaps the most important of the Lightning variants was the P-38L. Equipped with more powerful 1,600 hp engines and various other upgrades, it was considered by many to be the best of the breed. Over thirty-eight hundred were completed by the war's end.

The last noteworthy production P-38 variant was the P-38M Night Fighter. This was one of the first radar-equipped U.S. fighters ever, and was distinctive in having an elevated rear seat and associated extended rear canopy for a second crewmember.

The Champlin Collection P-38L was actually one of the very last Lightnings produced. It was a P-38M when delivered to the Air Corps, but after Champlin acquired it from Cecil Harp and Bob Ennis of Modesto, California in 1983, it was converted to its present P-38L single-seat configuration.

Messerschmitt Bf 109E-3

Manufacturer: Messerschmitt
Model: Bf 109E-3
Year: 1956
Registration: NX109J
Serial No.: c/n 186

Span: 32.38 feet
Length: 24.33 feet
Height: 7.46 feet
Wing Area: 174 square feet
Empty Weight: 4421 pounds
Gross Weight: 5523 pounds
Max Speed: 354 mph at 12, 300 feet
Max. Altitude: 37500 feet
Max. Range: 412 miles
Location: Champlin Fighter Museum
(Mesa, AZ)
Viewable

A Long and Varied Career

By far the most-produced fighter ever (over 33,000 estimated), the Bf 109 served actively in various air forces around the world from the mid-1930s until the mid-1950s. Small, agile, and well-armed, it proved a serious weapon in the hands of an experienced pilot. Perhaps the most noteworthy of the many versions of the Bf 109 was the Bf 109E, which ruled the skies over Europe until mid-1940 when the first Supermarine Spitfires appeared. The Bf 109 also had an extensive post-war career, being produced for and flying in several air forces other than the Luftwaffe. Most notable was front-line service with the Spanish and Czechoslovakian air forces, and later, the Israeli Air Force.

In 1972, Douglas Champlin began looking for a restorable Bf 109 for his collection. After several fruitless searches, he acquired a Spanish-built Hispano HA 1112 and reconfigured it as closely as possible to an original Bf 109E. This plane was manufactured in Germany in 1942 or 1943. It is thought to be one of the original batch of twenty-five aircraft supplied to Spain. All instrumentation is German, and of the identifiable Spanish-manufactured parts, many appear to be identical to the original German versions. Locating a Daimler-Benz DB-605 engine and associated cowling proved impossible, so a DB-601 was substituted. Appropriate to the aircraft's history, the cowling and engine are most likely from Bf 109E J392, the initial Dornier-Swiss-built aircraft delivered in 1945.

Modification work was undertaken by Art Williams in Germany. This included not only the engine change, but also redesign of the wingtips and other related items.

The Champlin Collection Bf 109 has appeared in several movies including *Patton* and *Battle of Britain*. Currently, the Bf 109E is displayed in the Battle of Britain colors of noted Luftwaffe ace, Hans "Assi" Hahn.

Aeronca L-3B

Manufacturer: Aeronca
Model: L-3B
Year: 1941
Registration: N47427, 9223
Serial No.: None

Span: 35 feet
Length: 21 feet
Height: 7.667 feet
Wing Area: 158 square feet
Empty Weight: 865 pounds
Gross Weight: 1850 pounds
Max Speed: 87 mph
Service Ceiling: 7750 feet
Range: 350 miles
Location: Museum of Flight
Viewable

L Is for Liaison

Aeronca's L-3 was a military version of the Model 65TC Defender. Modified with a wider fuselage, bigger windows, and military equipment, the L-3B was used as a patrol plane, VIP transport, and artillery spotter and director.

Adapt and Build

The Army's liaison planes weren't built from scratch. They were adapted and modified versions of civilian light planes. Using established designs and proven airframes saved time and money and brought the little planes into service fast. The Aeronca L-3B is an example of the light planes used by the Army during World War II. Piper, Taylorcraft, and Aeronca all got into the act: The Piper J-3 Cub became the L-4, Taylorcraft's Model D was the L-2, and Aeronca's Model 65TC Defender flew as the L-3. The Army's idea of using proven designs didn't stop there, they asked all three companies to make glider versions of the planes for training. Aeronca's three seat TG-5 glider had L-3 wings, tail sections, and rear fuselage with a redesigned glider nose

Send Grasshopper

The famous nickname of the Army's liaison planes came about in the summer of 1942 when Piper pilot Henry Wann was directed to fly a message from Fort Bliss, Texas to Cavalry Major General Innis Swift at his field headquarters. The General saw Wann's rough landing in a field and commented, "You looked like a damned grasshopper when you landed in those boondocks and bounced around!" Later, when Swift wanted Wann and his little plane to return, he sent a message to Fort Bliss, "Send Grasshopper." Bliss' personnel were baffled until Wann told them the story. Soon, all of the Army's liaison aircraft were called Grasshoppers.

Flight Fact: Some Aeronca L-3s weren't made for the Army—they were commandeered. At least forty-eight privately owned Aeroncas became L-3s after the U.S. entered the war.

The Museum's L-3B is one of about 8,900 Aeronca L-3s, Taylorcraft L-2s, and Piper L-4s made during World War II. It was purchased by Aeronca, Inc. in 1985, and was restored in its wartime colors for the Museum of Flight.

Goodyear FG-1D Corsair

Manufacturer: Goodyear
Model: FG-1D Corsair
Year: 1945
Registration: None
Serial No.: 88382

Span: 41 feet
Length: 33.33 feet
Height: 15 feet
Wing Area: 314 square feet
Empty Weight: 8694 pounds
Gross Weight: 11093 pounds
Max Speed: 415 mph
Service Ceiling: 37000 feet
Range: 1015 miles
Location: Museum of Flight
Viewable

Powerful and Versatile

The Chance Vought F4U Corsair was the premier Navy and Marine fighter of World War II. The Corsair and the Grumman Hellcat are credited with turning the tide of the Pacific air war by overwhelming the once-fearsome Japanese Zero fighter. Corsairs were used as fighter-bombers near the end of WW II and throughout the Korean War. The Corsair had an unusually long production run for a WW II-era aircraft with 12,571 produced, the last in 1952.

Bent Wing Bird

Chance Vought designer Rex B. Beisel, a graduate of Seattle's Queen Anne High School and the University of Washington, designed the Corsair around a large engine and massive propeller. Instead of building long, awkward landing gear needed for propeller clearance, Beisel's bent-wing design allowed for shorter, stronger gear for carrier landings. The unusual wing not only gave the Corsair its distinctive shape, but also reduced drag, allowing the Bent Wing Bird even greater speed.

Baa-Baa Black Sheep

One of the most famous squadrons to fly the Corsair was the Marine Corps Black Sheep squadron (VMF-214), commanded by Major Gregory "Pappy" Boyington. Pappy scored twenty-two victories over the Pacific in his Marine Corps Corsair. In early 1944 he was shot down and spent the final twenty months of WW II as a prisoner of war. Baa-Baa Black Sheep, the 1970s NBC series, presented Boyington's exploits to a new generation.

Flight Fact: The Corsair's propeller measures over 13 feet 4 inches (4 m)!

The Museum's Corsair was built under license by the Goodyear Company in April 1945 and served aboard the USS *Intrepid*. After the war, it was transferred to the Naval Reserve, eventually stationed at Naval Air Station-Sand Point, Seattle, Washington, in 1950. That July, Commander Ralph Milleson made a water landing on Lake Washington following a non-fatal midair collision with another Corsair. The aircraft was recovered from the lake in 1983 and restored.

This aircraft is on loan from the Naval Inventory Control Point at Philadelphia, PA.

Boeing B-17F Flying Fortress

Manufacturer: Boeing
Model: B-17F Flying Fortress
Year: 1943
Registration: N17W
Serial No.: 42-29782

Span: 103.75 feet
Length: 74.75 feet
Height: 19.2 feet
Wing Area: 1420 square feet
Empty Weight: 35728 pounds
Gross Weight: 48720 pounds
Max Speed: 325 mph at 25,000 feet
Service Ceiling: 37500 feet
Max. Range: 4420 miles
Location: Hangared
(Renton, WA)
Not Viewable

America's Queen of the Skies

The B-17 Flying Fortress served the Allied cause around the globe during World War II. Perhaps most famous for its Eighth Air Force raids on Germany and occupied territories, the B-17 was legendary for its ability to take punishment and return with its crew. Over 12,700 of Boeing's long-range bombers were built by men and women in U.S. factories by the end of the war.

Drawing Board Heroes

The B-17 was built to be tough. From the beginning, Boeing's President Claire Egtvedt had envisioned the bomber as an "aerial battleship." During the war, many B-17s limped home with terrible damage that would have most certainly destroyed lesser aircraft. Much of the credit goes to a young Boeing engineer named Ed Wells who worked on the bomber's preliminary design. Wells converted Egtvedt's ideas into the brawny bomber that brought aircrews home alive.

The Museum's carefully restored aircraft is the only flyable B-17F model left in the world. During World War II, it served as a stateside crew trainer. After the war, the plane was used as a chemical sprayer and fire bomber. The Fortress also appeared in movies—including *The Thousand Plane Raid* (1968), *Tora, Tora, Tora* (1969), and *Memphis Belle* (1989)—during its flying career.

Boeing B-29 Superfortress

Manufacturer: Boeing
Model: B-29 Superfortress
Year: 1945
Registration: None
Serial No.: 44-69729

Span: 140.23 feet
Length: 99 feet
Height: 27.75 feet
Wing Area: 1739 square feet
Empty Weight: 69610 pounds
Gross Weight: 140000 pounds
Cruise Speed: 220 mph
Max Speed: 365 mph
Service Ceiling: 31850 feet
Range: 5830 miles
Location: Museum of Flight
Viewable

A Superior Bomber

The B-29 Superfortress was the result of an effort to create a bomber with greater range and improved features. Being the first pressurized bomber and boasting a range and capacity far superior to existing aircraft, the first B-29s swung into action in June 1944 and were soon an integral part of the war in the Pacific. Two B-29s made history in August 1945 when they dropped atomic bombs on Hiroshima and Nagasaki, essentially ending the war.

The Museum's B-29 was assigned to the 498th Bomb Group (the 875th Bomb Squadron) and completed thirty-seven bombing missions in World War II, and was then converted to KB-29 (aerial refuelling tanker) in June 1949.

This B-29 is on loan from the U.S. Air Force Museum.

Republic P-47D Thunderbolt

Manufacturer: Republic
Model: P-47D Thunderbolt
Year: 1942
Registration: NX14519
Serial No.: 42-8205

Span: 40.78 feet
Length: 36.15 feet
Height: 14.58 feet
Wing Area: 300 square feet
Empty Weight: 10000 pounds
Gross Weight: 17500 pounds
Max Speed: 426 mph at 30,000 feet
Max. Altitude: 42000 feet
Max. Range: 1800 miles
Location: Champlin Fighter Museum
(Mesa, AZ)
Viewable

The Thunder Rolls

Republic's immense and powerful P-47 Thunderbolt was one of the truly great fighters of World War II. Two versions of the ubiquitous P-47D were manufactured. One, referred to as the Razorback, had a faired-in cockpit and canopy, and the other, known as the Bubble, had no canopy fairing and a bubble-type canopy offering a greatly improved field of view. All-told, an amazing 12,962 P-47Ds of both types eventually rolled from Republic's production lines on Long Island, New York.

In combat, the P-47 was an effective air-to-air fighter—but it was an even more effective air-to-ground weapon. It had great diving speed and a tremendous payload capacity. Some 5,222 P-47s were lost during the war, but only 3,499 of the losses were directly attributable to enemy action. Some 1,350,000 combat sorties were flown with a combat loss rate per sortie of just .7 percent.

He Made His Mark

Designed by Alexander Kartveli, who earlier had acquired a stellar reputation for designing great aircraft under the Seversky banner, the P-47 played a major role in World War II and was built in greater numbers than any other U.S. fighter, including the North American P-51.

The Champlin Museum's P-47D is a re-imported aircraft representing just one of the many Thunderbolts that were sent to Latin American countries as part of post-war military assistance programs. For a number of years, the Champlin Collection P-47D was a gate guardian at the La Paz, Bolivia airport. Doug Champlin acquired the aircraft from Jim Cullen in 1976 and shipped it off to Dick Martin of Carlsbad, California for a complete rebuild, which was completed in 1981. The aircraft is painted in the markings of Col. Robert Baseler's 325th Fighter Group aircraft (famous for their "checker tail" vertical tail paint scheme).

Supermarine Spitfire Mk.IX

Racing Plane Goes to War

Derived from the R.J. Mitchell-designed Schneider Cup racers of the 1920s and 1930s, Supermarine's immortal Spitfire came to life during the mid-1930s—unquestionably the most important British fighter of World War II and the symbol of the Battle of Britain. With its slim profile and elliptical wings, the Spitfire is definitely one of the most elegant fighter designs ever to grace the skies The first Spitfire flew in 1936 and by the beginning of World War II the type was in limited production.

Growing Up

Early Spitfires met their match in the Me 109, and later, the Focke Wulf Fw 190, but steady improvements in the airframe and engine eventually created a fighter that was the equal of anything the Axis could throw into the sky. One of the most important piston-engine fighters of all time, the most successful of the many Spitfire variants was the Mk.IX, the result of mating a Merlin 60 Series engine with the basic Spitfire VC airframe. The Spitfire Mk.IX type was produced in greater numbers than any other variant with 5,665 manufactured.

The Champlin Collection Mk.IX actually saw combat. Manufactured in late 1943, it first served with the Free French and participated in the June 1944 Normandy Invasion. After the war it was converted to a two-seat trainer for Ireland. Many years later, it was formally retired from the Irish Air Force in January 1960 with 1,402 hours in its logbook. In 1968, this aircraft participated in the filming of the movie *Battle of Britain*. Following a landing mishap in Amarillo, Texas during July 1968, it underwent a five-year restoration program and became part of the W. J. D. Roberts collection. Doug Champlin acquired this Spitfire from Roberts in 1974 and following a ground-loop during delivery to Mesa, Arizona in 1980, it was restored back to its original single-seat fighter configuration with RAF markings.

Manufacturer: Supermarine
Model: Spitfire Mk.IX
Year: 1943
Registration: N8R
Serial No.: MJ772

Span: 32.58 feet
Length: 31.33 feet
Height: 12.6 feet
Wing Area: 231 square feet
Empty Weight: 5800 pounds
Gross Weight: 7500 pounds
Max Speed: 404 mph at 21000 feet
Max. Altitude: 42500 feet
Max. Range: 980 miles
Location: Champlin Fighter Museum
(Mesa, AZ)
Viewable

Yakovlev Yak-9U

A Swarm of Light Planes

Developed from the earlier Yakovlev fighters that included the successful Yak-3 and Yak-7, the Yak-9 was simply a lighter version of the former. The single engine Yak-9 was optimized for ground attack with a wide variety of armament for use in anti-tank, light bomber and long-range escort roles, first seeing combat in 1942. The Yak-9 eventually was built in many different versions and a record 16,769 Yak-9's of all models were produced.

The Champlin Collection Yak-9 is a rare, rebuilt original aircraft, one of four original aircraft known and the only original Yak-9 on display in the west. Doug Champlin first learned of it during a trip to Russia in 1992, and hired Art Williams to find and acquire it. Williams traveled to Novosibirsk, Siberia, made the acquisition, and arranged for the Yak-9 to be transferred to Moscow on the Siberian railroad. The trip took four days under constant guard. Once the Yak-9 was in Moscow, Sergei Kotov arranged for a restoration team to rebuild it, which took two years to complete and in 1996, the Yak-9 was shipped to Mesa, Arizona.

This Yak-9 is equipped with an original engine and propeller, and all instrumentation and other miscellaneous parts are of original Russian manufacture. It is painted in the markings of Russian World War II ace, General Maesky.

Manufacturer: Yakovlev
Model: Yak-9U
Year: 1946
Registration: None
Serial No.: None

Span: 31.96 feet
Length: 28.42 feet
Height: 9.83 feet
Wing Area: 184.6 square feet
Empty Weight: 5988 pounds
Gross Weight: 6830 pounds
Max Speed: 434 mph
Max. Altitude: 39040 feet
Max. Range: 541 miles
Location: Champlin Fighter Museum
(Mesa, AZ)
Viewable

Goodyear F2G-1 Super Corsair

Manufacturer: Goodyear
Model: F2G-1 Super Corsair
Year: 1945
Registration: NX4324
Serial No.: None

Span: 41 feet
Length: 33.75 feet
Height: 16.08 feet
Wing Area: 314 square feet
Empty Weight: 10249 pounds
Gross Weight: 15422 pounds
Max Speed: 431 mph at 16400 feet
Max. Altitude: 38800 feet
Max. Range: 1955 miles
Location: Champlin Fighter Museum
(Mesa, AZ)
Viewable

The Super Bird

The Goodyear-built F2G was the ultimate permutation of Vought's Bent Wing Bird (the F4U Corsair). The Super Corsair was optimized for low-altitude operations and high-speeds and powered by the largest production piston engine ever manufactured in the U.S.—the twenty-eight cylinder Pratt & Whitney R-4360 air-cooled radial. The primary purpose of the F2G was to intercept and destroy Japanese suicide aircraft. Eventually, due to the cessation of hostilities, the contracts for the F2G-series were terminated and only ten (five F2G-1s and five F2G-2s) were actually completed.

The Champlin Collection F2G-1, the first production aircraft, was placed in storage after undergoing testing in 1945. With only 246 hours of flying time, it was in excellent condition. Following its rediscovery at Norfolk Naval Air Station in the late 1960s, a series of trades with the Marine Corps resulted in its initial refurbishment and delivery to Champlin's facility where further restoration was undertaken, including painting in the wartime colors of the Patuxent River Naval Air Test Center where most of its flying time had been accumulated.

Boeing WB-47E Stratojet

The Swept-Wing Way

Distinguished by 35-degree swept wings, pod-mounted multiple engines, and bicycle landing gear, Boeing introduced a design configuration that was a daring departure from existing designs for large aircraft. This design eventually became the standard for all modern jetliners and the B-47 Stratojet remains one of the most important aircraft ever designed by The Boeing Company.

SAC's Cold War Bomber

During the Cold War in the 1950s, the B-47 Stratojet became the backbone of the Strategic Air Command (SAC) medium bomber fleet. The B-47 needed defensive armament only in the rear because no fighter was fast enough to attack from any other angle. Aside from its lasting contribution to commercial aviation, the B-47 will be remembered as a primary deterrent to nuclear war at a time when that possibility was most threatening. Between 1947 and 1956, a total of 2,032 B-47s in all variants were produced by Boeing, Lockheed, and Douglas.

After serving in SAC from 1953 to 1963, the Museum's B-47 flew on weather reconnaissance missions overseas.

This aircraft is on loan from the Naval Inventory Control Point at Philadelphia, PA.

Manufacturer: Boeing
Model: WB-47E Stratojet
Year: 1951
Registration: None
Serial No.: 51-7066

Span: 116 feet
Length: 107 feet
Height: 27.92 feet
Wing Area: 1428 square feet
Empty Weight: 80756 pounds
Gross Weight: 220000 pounds
Cruise Speed: 495 mph
Max Speed: 606 mph
Service Ceiling: 40500 feet
Range: 4000 miles
Location: Museum of Flight
Viewable

Boeing B-52G Stratofortress

Manufacturer: Boeing
Model: B-52G Stratofortress
Year: 1959
Registration: None
Serial No.: 59-2584

Span: 185 feet
Length: 159.41 feet
Height: 40.67 feet
Wing Area: 4000 square feet
Take-off Weight: 488000 pounds
Gross Weight: 488000 pounds
Cruise Speed: 650 mph
Max Speed: 650 mph
Service Ceiling: 50000 feet
Range: More than 10000 miles
Location: Storage
Not Viewable

Back to the Drawing Board

The B-52, an eight-engine, 390,000-pound jet, had a rocky beginning. The original XB-52 design, selected by the Army Air Force in 1946, was for a straight-wing, six-engine, propeller-powered heavy bomber. On October 21, 1948, Boeing Chief Engineer Ed Wells and his design team were in Dayton, Ohio, when the Air Force's chief of bomber development told them to scrap the propellers and come up with an all-jet bomber. Over the weekend, in a Dayton hotel room, the team designed a new eight-engine jet bomber, still called the B-52, made a scale model out of balsa wood, and prepared a thirty-three-page report.

This effort impressed the Air Force's Air Material Command, and the design was approved. During 1951, as the war worsened in Korea, the Air Force designated the B-52 the country's next intercontinental bomber and approved an initial production order for thirteen B-52s. The first B-52A flew Aug. 5, 1954.

A Myriad of Uses

What began as an intercontinental, high-altitude nuclear bomber, the B-52's operational capabilities were adapted to meet changing defense needs as they have been modified for low-level flight, conventional bombing, extended-range flights, and transport of improved defensive and offensive equipment—including ballistic missiles that can be launched hundreds of miles from their targets. Some had photographic reconnaissance or electronic capsules in their bomb bays. The B-52s increased in range, power and capability with each variant. The B-52H made its first flight March 6, 1961, and is still in service. Between 1952 and 1962, a total of 744 B-52s were produced by The Boeing Company's Seattle and Wichita plants.

Throughout the 1950s, the B-52 chalked up numerous distance and speed records. It cut the round-the-world speed record in half, and in January 1962, it flew 12,500 miles nonstop from Japan to Spain without refueling. This flight alone broke eleven distance and speed records. The B-52s saw active duty in the Vietnam War and were used in the Persian Gulf War in 1991.

This B-52 is on loan from the U.S. Air Force Museum.

Dornier Do 27

A New German Plane

In 1951 C. Dornier, Jr. led a group of engineers starting investigations on the construction of a light liason transport and survey aircraft The aircraft that developed was designated Do25 and two prototypes were built in Sevilla, Spain. The Dornier Do 27 was developed from the Do 25, and was the first post-war German design to attain mass production in West Germany. The first customer was the German Defense Ministry, which ordered 428 of the craft. Production continued until 1964, when there were 568 Do 27s.

Powered by a Lycoming GO-480-BI.A6 270 hp engine, this airplane has a top speed of 135 knots and a range of 470 nautical miles. The Do 27 is useful on short runways, with a takeoff run of less than 300 feet, obtained by the use of leading edge slats and trailing edge double-slotted flaps.

The Museum's Do 27 was restored and donated by Dornier Reparaturwerft GmbH in Germany and brought to the U.S. by the Flying Tigers.

Manufacturer: Dornier
Model: Do 27
Year: 1956
Registration: None
Serial No.: None

Span: 39.38 feet
Length: 31.5 feet
Height: 9.17 feet
Wing Area: 208.8 square feet
Empty Weight: 2490 pounds
Gross Weight: 4070 pounds
Cruise Speed: 130 mph
Max Speed: 141 mph
Service Ceiling: 10825 feet
Range: 685 miles
Location: Restoration Center
(Everett, WA)
Not Viewable

Grumman F9F-8 Cougar

Manufacturer: Grumman
Model: F9F-8 Cougar
Year: 1953
Registration: None
Serial No.: 31232

Span: 34.5 feet
Length: 42.17 feet
Height: 12.25 feet
Wing Area: 337 square feet
Empty Weight: 11866 pounds
Max Weight: 24763 pounds
Cruise Speed: 516 mph
Max Speed: 647 mph
Service Ceiling: 42000 feet
Range: 1208 miles
Location: Museum of Flight
Viewable

Jet Cat

The F9F Cougar is the swept-wing version of its forerunner, the F9F Panther—Grumman's first jet fighter plane. As MiG-15s tangled over Korea with the slower, less agile Panthers and McDonnell Banshees, the Navy requested a swept-wing design from Grumman. The first Cougars were delivered in November 1951, a year after the debut of the MiG-15 and too late to see combat in Korea. But the Cougar, built as a stop-gap, became a successful design with 1,988 built. The last Cougar, an advanced trainer version, was phased out in 1974.

Look closely at any U.S. aircraft carrier deck from the 1930s to the 1990s and you'll see Grumman hardware. The "Grumman Iron Works" has been a dominant force in the supply of airplanes for the Navy for over sixty years, especially fighters. Grumman's famous "cat" series of fighters started with the Wildcat and Hellcat of World War II fame. The Grumman Tigercat and Bearcat came next and the jet-powered Panther flew in combat over Korea. Then the Cougar and the experimental Jaguar appeared. In the mid-1950s came the Tiger and, possibly the last of Grumman's famous cats, the F-14 Tomcat—seen in the movie *Top Gun*—took to the skies in 1970.

Corwin "Corky" Meyer

Corky Meyer joined Grumman in 1942 as an experimental test pilot. Over his fifty-five years of test flying, he piloted more than 125 types of civilian and military aircraft; including a Japanese Zero. In 1954, Meyer became the first civilian pilot to carrier-qualify aboard the USS *Lake Champlain*, flying a Grumman F9F Cougar. In 1997, he was awarded the coveted wings of gold from the Navy, which recognized Meyer for his lifelong contributions to Naval Aviation and named him an Honorary Naval Aviator—only the twenty-third in the U.S. Navy's history.

Flight Fact: Three Cougars set the transcontinental speed record in 1954 with a 2,438-mile (3, 900 km) flight in just over three hours and forty-five minutes, refueling over Kansas.

The Museum's Cougar was built at Grumman's Bethpage, New York factory and delivered to the Navy on January 25, 1955. The plane served with Navy and Marine units in North Carolina, Virginia, and Texas. In 1964, it was loaned to the King County Parks and Recreation Department and put on display at Marymoor Park. The Parks Department transferred the Cougar to the Museum of Flight in 1969. It is painted in the colors of Navy Fighter Squadron VF-81. This aircraft is on loan from the Naval Inventory Control Point at Philadelphia, PA.

Canadair CL-13B Sabre

Jet Fighter

The F-86 Sabre, designed by North American Aviation and built under license in Japan, Italy, Canada and Australia, is best known for its outstanding combat performance during the Korean War. First flown in 1947, the Sabre was the United States' first fighter to fly supersonic—in a dive. Starting in December 1950, the Russian-made MiG-15 and the F-86 met in combat over Korea. With superior aircraft performance, training and experience, Sabre pilots posted a ten-to-one victory ratio over the similar MiG-15. The last U.S. Sabre was retired from the Air National Guard in 1965.

Canada: Coast-to-Coast

In 1956, Canadian Sabre pilots set out to break the cross-Canada speed record held by a Royal Canadian Navy T-33. R.J. "Chick" Childerhose and Ralph Annis refueled halfway, in Gimli, Manitoba. The 1,400-mile (2,240 km) second leg from Gimli to Halifax stretched the Sabre's range to the limit. While test-flying that leg, Annis landed in Halifax with eight gallons of fuel. Childerhose had five. Yet the official cross-Canada dash went off without a hitch. The Sabres, flying on fumes, arrived in Halifax five hours after takeoff from Vancouver, shattering the old record by an hour and twenty minutes.

The Museum's example, a CL-13B, is one of 1,815 Sabres built by Canadair in Montreal. It flew with the Royal Canadian Air Force until 1974, then served The Boeing Company as a chase plane for their flight test division until donated to the Museum of Flight in 1991.

Manufacturer: Canadair
Model: CL-13B Sabre
Year: 1954
Registration: N8686F
Serial No.: 23363

Span: 37.96 feet
Length: 37.5 feet
Height: 14.75 feet
Wing Area: 302.3 square feet
Empty Weight: 10618 pounds
Gross Weight: 14613 pounds
Cruise Speed: 489 mph
Max Speed: 606 mph
Service Ceiling: 54000 feet
Range: 363 miles
Location: Museum of Flight
Viewable

Fiat G.91 PAN

Manufacturer: Fiat
Model: G.91 PAN
Year: 1956
Registration: NC10
Serial No.: MM 6244

Span: 29.54 feet
Length: 38.29 feet
Height: 14.5 feet
Wing Area: 195.15 square feet
Empty Weight: 8375 pounds
Gross Weight: 19180 pounds
Max Speed: 715 mph
Service Ceiling: 50000 feet
Range: 2175 miles
Location: Museum of Flight
Viewable

Italy's Lightweight Fighter

The Fiat G.91 design was the winner of a competition organized by NATO in the mid-1950s for a fast tactical fighter/ bomber airplane, with good general performance and good handling. It was capable of operating from prepared runways or grass fields, and had a low cost of maintenance. Several features—especially the swept wings, tail, and fuselage structure—bear a great resemblance to North American Aviation's F-86 Sabre. As recently as the mid-1990s, G.91s were still being flown by the air forces of Italy and other European countries.

PAN stands for Pattuglia Acrobatica Nationale (national aerobatic team). This flight demonstration group flew G.91s from 1963 to 1981. The Museum's Fiat G.91 PAN was one of several G.91s used by Frecce Tricolori—similar to the Blue Angels. It was donated to the Museum of Flight by Aeritalia— Societa Aerospatiale Italiana.

Source: Green/Swanborough, Complete Book of Fighters, *Salamander, 2001.*

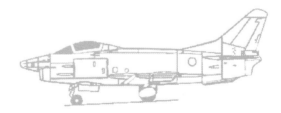

Vought XF8U-1 Crusader

Manufacturer: Vought
Model: XF8U-1 Crusader
Year: 1955
Registration: None
Serial No.: 138899

Span: 35.67 feet
Length: 54.33 feet
Height: 15.67 feet
Wing Area: 375 square feet
Empty Weight: 15513 pounds
Gross Weight: 26969 pounds
Max Speed: 1013 mph
Service Ceiling: 42300 feet
Combat Range: 398 miles
Location: Restoration Center
(Everett, WA)
Viewable

Born a Champion

The Navy was pleased with the Crusader from the start. On its maiden flight in 1955, this aircraft, the XF8U-1 prototype, exceeded Mach 1. In the years following, the Crusader would win the Collier Trophy for the year's greatest achievement in aviation, become the first fighter to fly over 1,000 miles-per-hour (1,600 kmph), and set the cross-country speed record with young Marine aviator, John Glenn, Jr. as pilot.

One unique feature of the F-8's design was the variable incident wing. Hinged to provide greater lift on take-off and landing, the wings could be tilted upward seven degrees. The radical design helped the fast jet fighter maintain the slow speeds required for carrier landings.

"Hey! Put Those Down!"

The Crusader had a unique characteristic unforeseen by its builders. It could fly with its wings folded. Although never deliberately tried, there are many accounts of the accidental take-offs with a "shorter" wingspan. Luckily, with the large center wing area and control surfaces inboard of the fold, most of these amazing flights ended with reasonably safe landings and very nervous pilots.

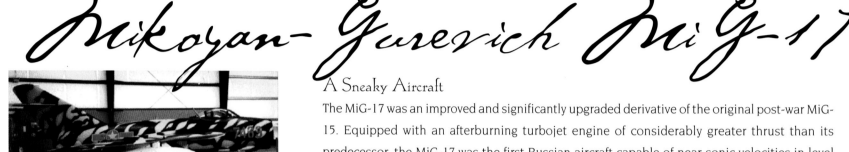

Mikoyan-Gurevich MiG-17

Manufacturer: Mikoyan-Gurevich
Model: MiG-17
Year: 1952
Registration: IFJ-10
Serial No.: 1406016

Span: 31.59 feet
Length: 36.39 feet
Height: 12.48 feet
Wing Area: 243.27 square feet
Empty Weight: 8664 pounds
Gross Weight: 11773 pounds
Max Speed: 711 mph at 9840 feet
Max. Altitude: 54500 feet
Max. Range: 913 miles
Location: Champlin Fighter Museum
(Mesa, AZ)
Viewable

A Sneaky Aircraft

The MiG-17 was an improved and significantly upgraded derivative of the original post-war MiG-15. Equipped with an afterburning turbojet engine of considerably greater thrust than its predecessor, the MiG-17 was the first Russian aircraft capable of near-sonic velocities in level flight. It could, in fact, fly supersonically in a shallow dive. Numerous versions of the MiG-17 were manufactured in Russia and several satellite countries.

The MiG-17 has served in the air forces of at least twenty nations throughout the world—including nations friendly to the U.S.—and was flown against U.S. aircraft during the Vietnam War. Lesser air combat events have since utilized the type in the Middle East and other parts of the world.

Flight Fact: Like a shark, the MiG-17 attacked from underneath the belly of its aircraft victim, with no radar warning.

The Champlin Collection MiG-17 is an early production version formerly active with the Moroccan Air Force. It was brought to the U.S. through the efforts of Maj. Gen. "Boots" Blesse, former president of the American Fighter Aces Association, and Col. Maj. Kabbaj, Royal Moroccan Air Force. The transfer to the Champlin Museum was formally approved by His Highness, King Hassan II in 1983. The MiG-17 was disassembled in Morocco and transported by C-130 and truck to Mesa, Arizona. It has been painted in the authentic camouflage markings of a North Vietnamese MiG-17F.

Lockheed F-104C Starfighter

The Starfighter

The F-104, America's first operational Mach 2 fighter, was built to counter the agile Soviet-built MiGs of the Korean War. The Starfighter, with its short wings and powerful engine, entered service with the U.S. Air Force in 1958 as an interceptor. By the Vietnam War, it had moved into a fighter/bomber role. The F-104 was immensely popular overseas with 2,578 Starfighters produced and well over half built under license in Canada, Europe, and Japan.

Jacqueline Cochran (Unknown—1980)

Jackie Cochran began her flying career in 1932 after only three weeks of instruction, and was soon winning air races, including the Bendix Trophy Race in 1938. During World War II, she organized and led the Women's Air Force Service Pilots (WASPs) and served as president of the International Organization of Women Pilots, called the Ninety-Nines (1941–1943). In the cockpit, Cochran won many awards and set numerous records, including a number of speed records in an F-104 in 1963 and 1964. Cochran was in her late fifties when she set her fastest record: 1,429 mph (2,286 kmph) over a 15 x 25 km course in a Starfighter.

"The Missile With a Man In It"

The Starfighter's design was quite radical. In fact, the F-104 program, led by the airframe design of Lockheed's Clarence "Kelly" Johnson, won the 1958 Collier Trophy for the year's outstanding aeronautical achievement. Johnson mated extremely small, thin wings to a powerful engine, producing a plane that was dubbed "the missile with a man in it." The design proved sound—the Starfighter was the first aircraft to simultaneously hold both the world speed and altitude records.

The Museum's F-104C was delivered to the U.S. Air Force in 1959. It has flown from George Air Force Base in California, Moron Air Base in Spain, and the Air Force Flight Test Center at Edwards Air Force Base. This Starfighter is painted to represent a NASA F-104.

This F-104C is on loan from the U.S. Air Force Museum.

Manufacturer: Lockheed
Model: F-104C Starfighter
Year: 1959
Registration: N56-934
Serial No.: 56-0934

Span: 21.75 feet
Length: 54.67 feet
Height: 13.42 feet
Wing Area: 196 square feet
Empty Weight: 12760 pounds
Max Weight: 27853 pounds
Cruise Speed: 510 mph
Max Speed: 1150 mph
Service Ceiling: 58000 feet
Range: 1500 miles
Location: Museum of Flight
Viewable

The Museum's plane is Northrop's prototype Freedom Fighter. It was unveiled on May 30, 1959 in front of visitors from forty foreign countries. Two months later, test pilot Lew Nelson flew the prototype supersonic during its first flight at Edwards Air Force Base.

Northrop YF-5A

Manufacturer: Northrop
Model: YF-5A
Year: 1959
Registration: None
Serial No.: 59-4987

Span: 25.25 feet
Length: 45.08 feet
Height: 13.08 feet
Wing Area: 170 square feet
Takeoff Weight: 12190 pounds
Cruise Speed: 88 mach
Max Speed: 1.3 mach
Service Ceiling: 55600 feet
Range: 2230 miles
Location: Museum of Flight
Viewable

Fighter for the Allies

In 1959, Northrop toured NATO and SEATO countries in Europe and Asia to determine their future aircraft needs. Their findings formed the basis for the N-156F—a simple, economical, versatile, and easy to maintain light fighter. In 1962, the aircraft was selected for use with the Mutual Assistance Pact (MAP) countries and designated the F-5A. The F-5 has been sold or produced in over thirty allied countries and also found favor in the U.S. Air Force and Navy as "a lot of airplane for a little price."

Aggressors

F-5Es became the "bad guys" for the Air Force's Red Flag and the Navy's Top Gun exercises. The shrinking victory-to-loss ratio of American pilots during Vietnam had both services looking to boost their pilot's air-to-air combat skills. The F-5, small and maneuverable, was quite similar to the Soviet MiG-21 encountered over Vietnam. Aggressor squadrons flying the F-5 and other Soviet-like aircraft in training helped American pilots post a 40-to-0 victory ratio over the Soviet-trained Iraqi pilots in 1991.

Jack Northrop (1895—1981)

John "Jack" Northrop joined the Loughead brothers company as a designer in 1916. After a brief time at Douglas, he helped establish the Lockheed Aircraft Company in 1927. Founding the independent Northrop Aircraft, Inc. in 1939, he built the world's first successful flying wing, America's first rocket-powered aircraft,

the JB-10 flying bomb, and the P-61 Black Widow night-fighter. After WW II, he co-founded Northrop Institute of Technology and built the XB-35 Flying Wing bomber. Northrop retired in 1952 but his company went on to design successful aircraft such as the Freedom Fighter, Talon trainer, and what later became the F/A-18 Hornet.

Flight Fact: A two-seat trainer version of Northrop's N-156F, called N-156T, was adopted by the Air Force and became the T-38 Talon even before the N-156F's first flight.

Douglas A-4F Skyhawk

Manufacturer: Douglas
Model: A-4F Skyhawk II
Year: 1966
Registration: 154180
Serial No.: None

Span: 27.5 feet
Length: 40.27 feet
Height: 15 feet
Wing Area: 260 square feet
Empty Weight: 10000 pounds
Gross Weight: 24500 pounds
Max Speed: 674 mph
Range: 2000 miles
Location: Museum of Flight
Viewable

"Heinemann's Hot Rod"

The nimble and speedy A-4 that wowed audiences with the Blue Angels for thirteen seasons bucked the trend that "bigger is better." In 1952, Douglas designer Ed Heinemann proposed that the Navy's newest attack plane be smaller, lighter, and faster than its contemporaries. Starting in 1956, the little but powerful A-4 flew with Navy and Marine units, including combat missions in Vietnam. The Skyhawk II had one of the longest production runs of any American combat aircraft, with 2,960 built over twenty-six years.

Edward Henry Heinemann (1908-1991)

Ed Heinemann became Chief Engineer at Douglas's El Segundo division in 1937. Over the next two decades, he designed many of the most famous Douglas military aircraft, such as the World War II-era A-20 Havoc, A-26 Invader, and SBD Dauntless dive bomber, plus the later AD-1 Skyraider and A-4 Skyhawk II. Heinemann was inducted into the National Aviation Hall of Fame in 1981 for his outstanding contributions to military aviation.

Mighty Mite

Ed Heinemann's A-4 design surpassed all of the Navy's requirements for a light attack aircraft at about half the requested size and weight. A little package with a powerful punch created many advantages over larger Navy planes. The A-4s were easy to manage on an aircraft carrier deck and their stubby modified delta wings didn't need to be folded for storage. Without the wing-folding mechanisms, the Skyhawk was even lighter and simpler to maintain—aspects that allowed it to stay in operational service for over thirty-five years.

The Museum's A-4 was built in 1967 and flew with the Navy in Southeast Asia. Active in Navy squadrons throughout the 1970s, the plane was transferred to the Blue Angels in 1980. This aircraft was often flown in the number four or "slot" position. When the Blues Angels fly in diamond formation, the slot flies directly behind the leader, surrounded on three sides by other aircraft.

This aircraft is on loan from the Naval Inventory Control Point at Philadelphia, PA.

McDonnell F-4C Phantom II

Manufacturer: McDonnell
Model: F-4C Phantom
Year: 1964
Registration: None
Serial No.: 64-0776

Span: 38.42 feet
Length: 58.31 feet
Height: 16.25 feet
Wing Area: 530 square feet
Empty Weight: 28496 pounds
Gross Weight: 51441 pounds
Cruise Speed: 587 mph
Max Speed: 1433 mph
Service Ceiling: 56100 feet
Range: 538 miles
Location: Museum of Flight
Viewable

Brutishly Ugly

The F-4 Phantom II, with its harsh symmetry, swept-back wings, and drooping tail was called "brutishly ugly" by some pilots. But whatever the Phantom lacked in looks, it more than made up for with exceptional performance. When unveiled, the fighter was considered huge and immensely powerful. In 1958, the F-4 was selected by the U.S. Navy as a fleet defense interceptor. Soon, its remarkable capabilities led the Air Force and Marine Corps to use it as well. As the pre-eminent American combat aircraft of the 1960s, it fulfilled the roles of interceptor, air superiority fighter, and reconnaissance aircraft for more than ten years. It became the standard by which all other fighters were judged.

Have Gun, Will Travel

The first F-4 Phantoms built by McDonnell didn't have a gun. Many designers and military thinkers of the late 1950s thought that a fighter's supersonic speeds and the development of air-to-air missiles would make the trusty gun, affixed to planes since World War I, obsolete. But over Vietnam, when a Phantom's high-tech missiles went on the blink or a MiG came in too close for comfort, a gun was a necessity. Some F-4s, like the Museum's C-model, were fitted with an exterior gun pod while later Phantoms had a gun built-in.

Flying by Team

Sophisticated radar and avionics on the F-4 require a two-man crew. American F-4 flyers in Vietnam soon found, in the high-speed world of jet dogfighting, that the backseater's second pair of eyes also gave the F-4 a distinct advantage over single-man MiG fighters. The team of Major Robert Anderson and Captain Fred Kjer scored this Phantom's first victory over a MiG-21 in April 1967. A month later, Lt. Colonel Robert Titus and 1st Lt. Milan Zimer scored two victories over MiG-21s on the same day in this aircraft.

Flight Fact: This F-4's combat victories all came using different weapons systems—one with an AIM-9 Sidewinder heat-seeking missile, one with an AIM-7 Sparrow radar-guided missile, and one with a 20mm gun pod.

The Museum's F-4C was built in 1965 and served in Vietnam. After its active Air Force duty, this Phantom served the Oregon Air National Guard for nine years, flying tactical defense exercises out of Portland International Airport. This F-4C is on loan from the U.S. Air Force Museum.

Blackbird—Mother Ship

The Blackbird family of aircraft cruise at speeds of more than Mach 3 and fly over 85,000 feet (25,500 m) in altitude. Conceived over thirty years ago, Blackbirds remain the fastest and highest flying air-breathing production aircraft ever built. Design features of the M-21 include the second seat for the Launch Control Officer and the launch pylon on which a drone is mounted.

Built for a CIA program code-named *Tagboard*, the M-21 carried unpiloted vehicles—D-21 drones. These drones were intended for launch from the M-21 mother ship for intelligence-gathering flights over hostile territories.

Clarence "Kelly" Johnson

When young engineer Kelly Johnson came to Lockheed in 1933, one of the first things he told his new employers was that their new airplane design, the Electra, was inherently unstable. Instead of being fired, Johnson was put to work on the problem. A double vertical tail configuration cured the Electra's woes and became a familiar trait of other Lockheed planes Kelly helped design, including the P-38 Lightning, the Lodestar, the Ventura, and the triple-tailed Constellation. In the early 1940s, Johnson established and led Lockheed's "Skunk Works"—an advanced development department that built some of America's most radical and fascinating aircraft including the P-80, the U-2, the F-104, and the Blackbird spyplane.

Revolutionary Design

In 1959, Lockheed's Skunk Works won the contract to build a new spy plane for the CIA and Air Force. Because of the extreme operating altitude, speeds, and temperatures, practically everything on the new Blackbird had to be "reinvented" including tires, oil, fuel, even paint. Kelly Johnson claimed that he offered fifty dollars to any one of his engineers that could find something easy or conventional to do on the project. "I might as well have offered a thousand dollars," he said, "because I still have the money." In spite of the difficulties, Lockheed prevailed. Within twenty-six months, the Skunk Works had developed hundreds of revolutionary components and a 95 percent titanium structure necessary to withstand the high temperatures of the Blackbird's Mach 3 flight.

Flight Fact: An SR-71, part of Lockheed's Blackbird family, set the world speed and altitude records for an air-breathing production plane. The records of 2,193 mph (3,509 kph) and 85,000 ft. (25,500 m) set in 1976, have never been broken.

Manufacturer: Lockheed
Model: M-21
Year: 1964
Registration: None
Serial No.: 60-6940

Span: 55.58 feet
Length: 102.25 feet
Height: 18.5 feet
Wing Area: 1795 square feet
Empty Weight: 52000 pounds
Gross Weight: 117000 pounds
Cruise Speed: 3 mach
Max Speed: still classified
Service Ceiling: still classified
Range: still classified
Location: Museum of Flight
Viewable

The Museum's M-21 mother ship was built in 1963, one of two A-12s modified to carry drones, and is on display with a D-21 drone mounted on it. It is the only surviving example of its type. During a launch test in 1966, a drone crashed into the other mother ship, which spun wildly out of control. Both crewmen ejected, but Launch Control Officer Ray Torick drowned in the Pacific. The failures caused Lockheed's Kelly Johnson to cancel the program. Later, D-21 drones were launched from B-52Hs until the early 1970s when the project was cancelled altogether.

Lockheed D-21

Manufacturer: Lockheed
Model: D-21B Drone
Year: 1964
Registration: None
Serial No.: 90-0510

Span: 19.02 feet
Length: 42.83 feet
Height: 7.02 feet
Gross Weight: 11000 pounds
Cruise Speed: 3.25 mach
Max Speed: 3.35 mach
Service Ceiling: 95000 feet
Range: 3000 miles
Location: Museum of Flight
Viewable

The D-21's Mission

The D-21 drone was an unpiloted aircraft originally designed for CIA and Air Force surveillance missions over hostile territories. Launched from airborne carrier aircraft, the D-21's ramjet engine propelled it at speeds over 2,000 miles per hour (3,200 kph). During a reconnaissance mission, the D-21 drone would follow a pre-programmed flight path over areas of interest. Then the drone would return to a "friendly" area where the reconnaissance data package could be ejected. The package was then recovered either in mid-air by a specially equipped airplane or at sea by a ship. Shortly after the data package was jettisoned, the drone self-destructed.

Runaway

Engineer Ben Rich worked on the D-21 program starting in 1962. Later, when he succeeded Kelly Johnson as the head of Lockheed's secret Skunk Works, he told of a day in the mid-1980s when a CIA man arrived carrying a panel. "Do you recognize this?" Rich did—but couldn't figure out how the CIA man had got it. "It was a Christmas gift from a Soviet KGB agent," the CIA man explained. "He told me it was found by a shepherd in Soviet Siberia." The panel was part of a D-21 drone that had disappeared during testing over China in 1969. Hopelessly off course, the D-21 ran out of fuel and crashed in Russia's vast frontier.

Flight Fact: After the drone the program was cancelled, the seventeen remaining drones were placed into storage at Davis-Monthan Air Force Base.

The two Lockheed M-21 mother ships were designated M-21/D-21s when the D-21 daughter drone was mounted on top, as displayed at the Museum.

This D-21 drone is on loan from the U.S. Air Force Museum.

Mikoyan-Gurevich MiG-21 PFM

Manufacturer: Mikoyan-Gurevich
Model: MiG-21 PFM (Fishbed)
Year: 1967
Registration: None
Serial No.: 5411

Span: 23 feet
Length: 47.5 feet
Height: 13.17 feet
Wing Area: 256 square feet
Empty Weight: 11420 pounds
Max Weight: 17086 pounds
Max Speed: 1352 mph
Service Ceiling: 60958 feet
Range: 1044 miles
Location: Museum of Flight
Viewable

NATO Code Name: "Fishbed F"

The MiG-21 is probably one of the best-known Soviet aircraft— flown by many nations and built in larger numbers than any warplane since World War II. It was designed in response to Korean War needs for a short-range interceptor and light strike fighter. First flown in 1955, the MiG-21 was Russia's first operational fighter capable of speeds in excess of Mach 2. For three decades, variants of the MiG-21 went head-to-head with the F-4 Phantom and other American-made fighters in Cold War-related conflicts throughout the world.

The Russian Equivalent

The Soviet "experimental construction bureau" ranks with The Boeing Company as one of the world's most famous and influential aircraft manufacturing organizations. Founded by designers Artyem Mikoyan and Mikhail Gurevich in 1939, MiG builds only fighters, creating many variants of a few basic designs. Mikoyan began design of the MiG-21 in 1953 and they continued to be built until the mid-1980s.

Simply a Fighter

Soviet fighters like the MiG-21 are designed and built differently from their Western counterparts. American fighters are large, sophisticated, two-engine, two-person aircraft designed to carry out many different missions. The MiG aircraft, on the other hand, are relatively small, defensive fighters built with traditional materials and simple manufacturing. Why make them basic? Soviet aircraft can be built quickly, inexpensively, and in large numbers. In combat, MiGs are tough, simple, rugged planes that can operate from unprepared airfields with minimum logistics support and can be maintained simply, by basically unskilled labor. Accordingly, several thousand remain in operation with small air forces across the globe.

Flight Fact: In the mid-1980s, MiG-21s were in service with at least thirty-seven air forces worldwide.

The Museum's MiG-21 was acquired from the Czech Republic after the breakup of the Soviet Union. Boeing employee Jim Blue discovered this MiG-21, along with about sixty others, destined for the scrap yard. Through generous donations of Blue and others, the MiG was purchased, shipped to Seattle, and reassembled at the Museum of Flight.

McDonnell AV-8C Harrier

The VTOL Jump

The vertical take-off (VTOL), thrust-vectored, jet-powered Harrier was one of the most dramatic developments in combat aircraft since the introduction of the turbojet at the end of World War II. The Harrier was developed from the Hawker Siddeley P.1127, the first aircraft to offer VTOL by means of thrust vectoring, which was demonstrated in October 1960. The first production Harriers flew in August 1966.

Adaptability Is the Key

The U.S. Marine Corps selected the Harrier as a close air support aircraft. Its ability to operate from ship decks or from rough landing sites made it attractive to the Marines for the support of its ground troops in beach-head assaults. In 1971, the Marines received the first of their AV-8A Harriers. In 1974 the Marine Corps issued requirements for an advanced Harrier, which led to the AV-8B Harrier II developed by McDonnell Douglas. Improvements included the use of a supercritical wing, a more powerful engine and electronic modernization.

The Museum's AV-8C Harrier was one of forty-seven AV-8As that were upgraded for the Marine Corps until the new Harrier IIs were ready to enter service. Upgrades included a more powerful engine, more sophisticated electronic equipment, and aerodynamic improvements. The Museum's aircraft entered service with Marine Corps squadron VMA-542 in 1986.

Manufacturer: Hawker Siddeley/McDonnell
Model: AV-8C Harrier (Converted from an AV-8A in 1979)
Year: 1973
Registration: None
Serial No.: 158977

Span: 25 feet
Length: 45 feet
Height: 11 feet
Empty Weight: 12100 pounds
Gross Weight: 25999 pounds
Maximum Weight: 26000 pounds
Max Speed: 737 mph
Location: Paine Field
Viewable

Grumman A-6E Intruder

Manufacturer: Grumman
Model: A-6E Intruder
Year: 1970
Registration: None
Serial No.: 158794

Span: 53 feet
Length: 54.75 feet
Height: 16.17 feet
Wing Area: 529 square feet
Empty Weight: 26746 pounds
Gross Weight: 60400 pounds
Cruise Speed: 474 mph
Max Speed: 644 mph
Service Ceiling: 42400 feet
Range: 3245 miles
Location: Museum of Flight
Viewable

The Old Workhorse

During the Korean Conflict, the U.S. needed rugged jet aircraft suited for attack missions. The A-6 was designed as a tough and versatile all-weather attack bomber to fill this role. Major improvements in avionics and hardware have made the Intruder the workhorse of the Navy and Marine Corps for over thirty years—from Vietnam to beyond Desert Storm.

The A-6E can deliver the Navy's entire arsenal of available air-to-ground weapons, from general purpose bombs to ground attack missiles, as well as air-to-air missiles. During the Vietnam War, the A-6's all-weather capability, long range, and tremendous payload represented a quantum leap in carrier-based power projection. An attack under cover of darkness by a pair of early model A-6s was assessed by the North Vietnamese to have been the work of B-52s.

The Museum's A-6E entered service in 1972. It has flown with nine Navy squadrons including bombing missions over Iraq during the Gulf War. This aircraft is on loan from the National Museum of Naval Aviation at Pensacola, Florida.

Boeing AGM-86B ALCM

Air Launch Cruise Missile

The ALCM is a small, unmanned air vehicle carried by the U.S. Strategic Air Command B-52 and B-1 bombers. Operational in late 1982, the cruise missile is called a "stand-off weapon" because of its ability to hit a target hundreds of miles away without endangering air crews. The unmanned ALCM can carry a nuclear or high explosive warhead over 1, 550 miles (2, 494 km).

The ALCM flies low, at treetop level, so as not to be detected and fired upon. It is guided by a computer that uses a radar altimeter to match the surrounding terrain with an electronic "map" of the ALCM's pre-planned route.

The Museum's AGM-86B mock-up was restored by the Auburn Chapter of the Boeing Management Association.

Manufacturer: Boeing
Model: ALCM
Year: 1979
Registration: None
Serial No.: Reproduction

Wing Span: 12 feet
Length: 19.5 feet
Diameter: 25 inches
Launch Weight: 2800 pounds
Top Speed: Subsonic
Range: 1550 miles
Location: Museum of Flight
Viewable

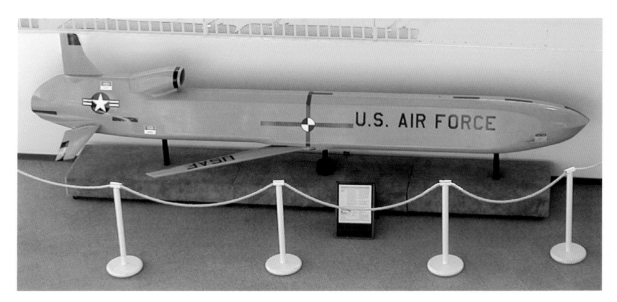

Grumman F-14A Tomcat

Necessity-Based Invention

Failure of the General Dynamics' F-111B to meet U.S. Navy requirements for an advanced, carrier-based, air superiority fighter led to a new design contest. This one was won by Grumman with the F-14, a variable geometry, two-seat, twin-engined aircraft named the Tomcat. Procurement began in 1969 for seven hundred aircraft. Deliveries to the Navy began in June 1972 with deployment of operational carrier squadrons in 1974.

Truly a Fighting Machine

With the ability to sweep its wings aft 43 degrees from the horizontal and twin 21,000-pound thrust engines, the F-14 achieves speeds over twice the speed of sound. Add to that, the F-14's Phoenix air-to-air missiles, coupled with airborne early warning radar, and you have a fighter that is able to simultaneously intercept, engage and destroy up to five incoming enemy aircraft out to distances in excess of five hundred miles from a carrier task force. The F-14 is now used in the attack role, as well.

Progress

Reduction of force requirements and concurrent cuts in defense spending has necessitated gradual replacement of the F-14s by F/A-18s by the year 2008.

This aircraft is on loan from the National Museum of Naval Aviation at Pensacola, Florida.

Manufacturer: Grumman
Model: F-14A Tomcat
Year: 1976
Registration: None
Serial No.: 160382

Span (swept): 33 feet
Span (extended): 64 feet
Length: 62 feet
Height: 16 feet
Wing Area: 565 square feet
Empty Weight: 40070 pounds
Gross Weight: 73349 pounds
Max Speed: 2.34 mach
Service Ceiling: 56100 feet
Range: 1000 miles
Location: Museum of Flight
Viewable

Piasecki H-21 B Workhorse

Manufacturer: Piasecki
Model: H-21B Workhorse
Year: 1951
Registration: N6797
Serial No.: 53-4366

Rotor Diameter: 44 feet
Length: 52.5 feet
Height: 16 feet
Empty Weight: 8906 pounds
Gross Weight: 15000 pounds
Cruise Speed: 101.2 mph
Max Speed: 117 mph
Service Ceiling: 10800 feet
Range: 500 miles
Location: Restoration Center
(Everett, WA)
Viewable

The Flying Banana

The H-21 was developed in 1949 as the HRP-2 for the United States Navy. In 1952 the United States Air Force ordered eighteen for trials. The H-21 was the first tandem-rotor helicopter delivered to the Air Force. Its odd shape prevents the rotors from interfering with one another and quickly earned it the nickname Flying Banana.

The aircraft was originally designed to transport men and cargo, but was later adapted for the rescue of personnel and for assault operations under combat conditions. These early helicopters were used as utility and rescue aircraft in the Korean War. They had inflatable pontoons on the wheels allowing the aircraft to land on water. Normally having a crew of two (pilot and copilot), the H-21 could carry either twenty fully-equipped troops or twelve litter patients. Considered to be the first heavy lift helicopter, a modified HU-21 made the first nonstop transcontinental helicopter flight on August 24, 1956.

Frank Piasecki

The designer, Frank Piasecki, was the first person in the United States to hold a commercial helicopter license. His aircraft company, Piasecki Aviation, changed its name to Vertol in 1956 and is still designing aircraft as a division of The Boeing Company.

Hiller YH-32 Hornet

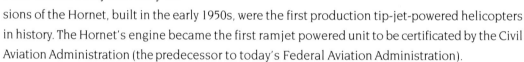

Manufacturer: Hiller
Model: YH-32 Hornet
Year: 1953
Registration: None
Serial No.: 55-4969

Rotor Diameter: 23 feet
Fuselage Width: 3.75 feet
Height: 8.33 feet
Empty Weight: 544 pounds
Loaded Weight: 1080 pounds
Cruise Speed: 69 mph
Service Ceiling: 6900 feet
Range: 28 miles
Location: Museum of Flight
Viewable

Where Is the Engine?

The small and simple YH-32 Hornet is unique because of the two ramjets mounted on the tips of its rotor blades. Army and Navy versions of the Hornet, built in the early 1950s, were the first production tip-jet-powered helicopters in history. The Hornet's engine became the first ramjet powered unit to be certificated by the Civil Aviation Administration (the predecessor to today's Federal Aviation Administration).

Two Little Ramjets

The two simple, 12.7 pound (5.72 kg) ramjet engines that noisily keep the Hornet flying have no moving parts and can be disassembled in minutes with only a screwdriver. How does a ramjet work? Air goes in the front and is compressed as the engine moves forward. The compressed air flows past a fuel spray nozzle and the mixture is ignited. Pressure from the burning fuel and air sends a flaming exhaust out the exit nozzle that pushes the engine forward.

The Museum's helicopter is one of twelve YH-32s acquired by the Army for evaluation in 1955. It was restored in 1989.

Sikorsky HH-52 Seaguard

Amphibious Jet

The HH-52 was specially designed to operate from land, sea or snow. It features a watertight flying-boat type hull that allows it to land on water as well as on dry ground. Two outrigger floats help stabilize the helicopter, keeping the helicopter upright in eight to ten foot seas. The HH-52 civilian version, the Sikorsky S-62, was the first jet-powered helicopter to be certified by the Federal Aviation Administration.

The Seaguard

The Sikorsky HH-52 Seaguard served as the Search and Rescue workhorse of the Coast Guard for over twenty-five years. The HH-52 is estimated to have saved more than 15,000 lives and $1.5 billion in property loss or damage since its deployment with the Coast Guard in 1963. Ninety-nine Seaguard helicopters were based at Coast Guard stations, cutters, and icebreakers until retirement in 1989.

Coast Guard Air Station Port Angeles, Washington

The Coast Guard has maintained a presence in Port Angeles since 1862, but air operations did not begin until the Air Station was commissioned in 1935. The station received its first helicopter in 1946, and since 1973 has flown helicopters exclusively. During a typical year, the Port Angeles Coast Guard Group carries out over four hundred missions, saving thirty-five lives and assisting five hundred persons.

Flight Fact: For every dollar spent to purchase HH-52s, the Coast Guard saved ten dollars in property.

The Museum's helicopter, Coast Guard Number 1415, entered service in 1966. It has since flown from Coast Guard Air Stations in Detroit, Michigan; Mobile, Alabama; Elizabeth City, North Carolina; and Cape May, New Jersey. Its last station was Port Angeles, Washington, where it flew from 1982 until retirement in 1988, when it was donated to the museum by the United States Coast Guard.

Manufacturer: Sikorsky
Model: HH-52 Seaguard
Year: 1963
Registration: CGNR1415
Serial No.: Unknown

Rotor Diameter: 53 feet
Length: 45.46 feet
Height: 14.21 feet
Empty Weight: 4903 pounds
Gross Weight: 8300 pounds
Cruise Speed: 98 mph
Max Speed: 109 mph
Service Ceiling: 11200 feet
Range: 474 miles
Location: Restoration Center
(Everett, WA)
Viewable

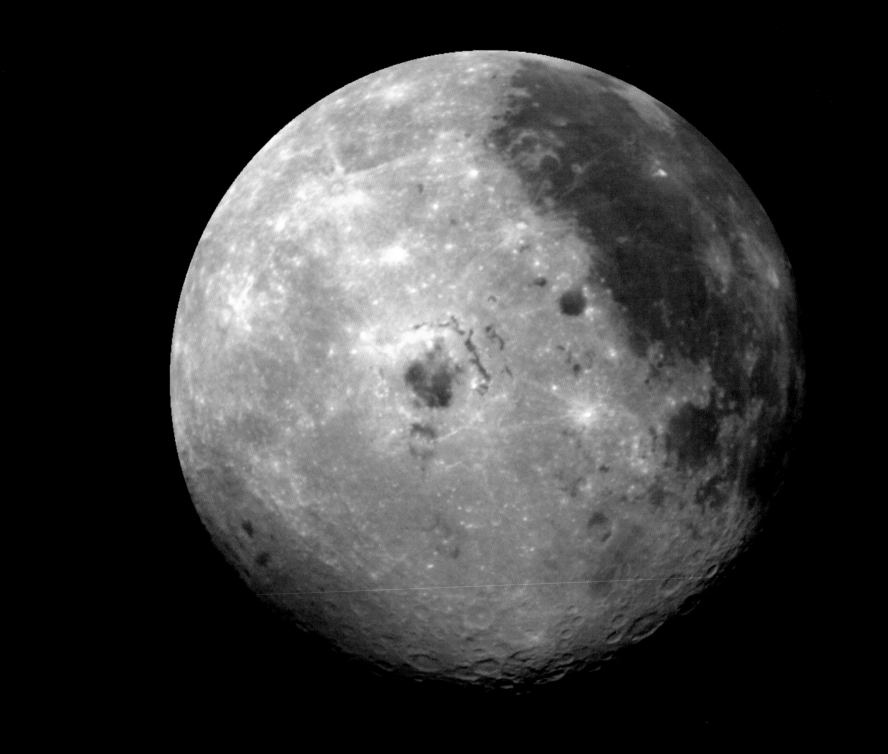

Space Craft

What are we doing here? We're reaching for the stars.

– *Christa McAuliffe*, Time Magazine, 1986

What is your favorite aircraft to fly?
The F-86 Sabre Jet was the most responsive and gave me the most satisfaction as far as feeling in control. The F-86 made a name for itself in the Korean War where it took on, and usually beat, the much-vaunted (and similar looking) Soviet MiG 15. With the F-86, I shot down two MiGs during the Korean War.

Who are your heroes in aviation?
My father was an aide to General Billy Mitchell. He was an influence on early military aviation as well as on me through my father's association. Another was Jimmy Doolittle who was a friend and contemporary of my dad and an advisor to me. Like Doolittle, I was fortunate to be in the right place at the right time. Another person I admire is Burt Rutan who designed a number of aircraft including the Voyager, which his brother flew around the world.

What was your initial reaction when you heard you were going to the moon (Apollo 11)?
It was progressive, a mix of guarded anticipation and expectation. There were gradual suspicions as time went on of who would go. The closer it got, the more you knew you were in the running. Crews were chosen for Apollo 8, 9, and 10. By January of 1969, as the backup crew for the successful Apollo 8 lunar Christmas mission, we were touted as being on the Apollo 11 crew. But that mission wasn't a sure thing until 9 and 10 were completed successfully. I heard years later that Frank Borman wrote in his book that the Apollo 8 crew was originally offered the Apollo 11 mission.

What was the most unexpected experience or observation on that trip?
The most unexpected and what caused a little trouble and threat to our success were the computer alarms going off during our power descent. The computer was slightly overloaded and the alarms were distracting, but not of serious significance.

Where do you think the space program would be if there had been no cutbacks?
I think the difficulty in creating a shuttle and space station program was underestimated; it was over-ambitious in some ways. The program was under-funded for the enormity of what was needed. We rushed into a program without laying out the most effective and long-term method to proceed. This was reflected in the catastrophe on Challenger. And, at the time and with the technology and funds available, we knew we couldn't sustain lunar landings.

Give one prediction for the future of space travel.
We'll have space tourism and visits to asteroids before people go to Mars. Space travel could be made more affordable and open to not just the rich but everyone through a lottery-type selection system. The U.S. is still leading the world in space. But space exploration and travel isn't just about science. It's about human involvement. And it takes that human involvement to get Congress behind it so that we can continue moving forward.
                                              —*Buzz Aldrin*, Astronaut Apollo 11, Commissioner on the Future of the U.S. Aerospace Industry

Bill Anders

Now, in the twenty-first century, it is sometimes hard to remember the very intense political, philosophical and military competition of the 1950s and 1960s. The Cold War was taken very seriously by the U.S. and our free world allies. When the U.S.S.R. launched the first earth-orbiting satellite, Sputnik, and then the first human, Yuri Gagarin, these space firsts made us question the strength of our country ' s political, economic and educational systems and our technology. These were dark times in America.

In response President John F. Kennedy announced on May 25, 1961, that America would "go to the moon in this decade…not because it is easy but because it is hard…." This excited the imagination and support of the American people in a way not seen since WW II, and NASA pulled together a team that led our country on its historic quest.

The U.S. manned lunar landing program had three phases. Phase one: the one-man Mercury capsule to show that humans could live and work in space. Phase two: the two-man Gemini to test the rendezvous and docking maneuvers for the lunar-orbit-rendezvous plan. Phase three: the three-man Apollo program for the lunar landing. Apollo hardware consisted of the giant Saturn V rocket (365 feet tall with 7.5 million pounds of thrust), the command and service modules to carry the three-man crew from earth to lunar orbit and back to earth; and the two-man lunar module for the lunar landing itself.

I was fortunate to be selected as one of fourteen Apollo astronauts. With eighteen others, selected earlier, we trained on spacecraft systems and procedures; jungle, ocean, and desert survival (in case of emergency landing); helicopters (for lunar descent training); and geology (to help explore the moon). Frank Borman, James Lovell and I were selected to fly Apollo 8. Originally planned as an earth-orbit test of the lunar module, plans changed in the fall of 1968 when U.S. intelligence suspected that the Soviets might attempt a manned lunar orbit in December. If successful, they would obtain another great PR coup over the U.S. in space. NASA reacted swiftly and decisively, switching the Apollo 8 mission to a lunar orbit mission, a very big change and gamble.

We launched on the first Saturn V on December 21, 1968. After two earth orbits we were hurled out of earth orbit at over 25,000 mph and off to a rendezvous with the moon—240,000 miles away—the first time humans had ever left Earth. After two and a half days we entered a 60-mile-high lunar orbit. We were thrilled with the views of the lunar orbit and even more so of our beautiful home planet. From lunar orbit on Christmas Eve we read the first verses from the book of Genesis ("In the beginning…") and I took the *Earthrise* picture, which has been selected as one of the ten most influential pictures of the twentieth century. Ironically, we came to study the moon, but it was the view of "the good earth"—so small, so beautiful, so fragile…like a Christmas tree ornament—that most moved us and our fellow humans.

Many thought Apollo was a program of exploration, science, and a demonstration of technological pre-eminence. Yes, it was all of those things, but, as Apollo 8 Commander Frank Borman insightfully reminds us, "…it was just another battle in the Cold War…." For me it was a chance to serve my country, and a real adventure.

—*Bill Anders*, Apollo 8 Astronaut

Pinky Nelson

Humans have reached for the stars for tens of thousands of years. In the last forty years we have taken our first small steps on that journey. In the 1950s there were two distinct approaches that have merged in today's space programs. The rocket planes like the X1 and the X15 were genuine flying machines built to take advantage of the human on board, but they could only reach the edge of space on their brief flights. Early manned space capsules, on the other hand, shared some systems and controls with airplanes but that may just reflect the heritage of their designers. Given the modest control that the capsule "pilots" had during their brief trips through the atmosphere it wouldn't have made much difference what the controls looked like. Though once they were lofted into the free-fall conditions of Earth or lunar orbit atop a booster rocket, the Mercury, Gemini, and Apollo craft were exquisitely maneuverable. The lunar lander, I think, belongs in a class by itself. A remarkable vehicle built for remarkable pilots to make one vertical landing and one take-off—on the moon.

The Space Shuttle is the first spacecraft to launch like a rocket, maneuver in space like the capsules, and glide like the X-vehicles. But there are still big differences between the shuttles and any airplane. Drastic measures are necessary to make one fly like the other. For example, to fly a final approach at the same speed (300 knots) and sink rate (11,000 feet per minute) as the shuttle, the Shuttle Training Aircraft, a modified business jet, climbs to 35,000 feet then puts down full flaps, lowers its main landing gear and pulls its engines into full reverse thrust. Piloting the shuttle during entry and landing is the ultimate test for any pilot. I am still in awe of my colleagues who make it look so routine.

My experience as the solo pilot of my own spacecraft, the Manned Maneuvering Unit is limited—about 45 minutes of actual flying time—but it was sublime. Imagine attaching a device to your life support backpack then undoing all of the tethers connecting you to the shuttle and stepping out of the foot restraints to become your own personal flying machine. The only instruments are two small tank pressure gauges and two lights that indicate "jet" firing commands. There is a translation controller in your left hand and a rotation controller in your right hand, plus some systems switches including an inertial hold button on the top of the left-hand controller. All navigation is done by sight. Even though I flew at small speeds relative to the shuttle and the satellite I was attempting to capture, I couldn't help but be aware that I was flying over the Earth at 17,500 miles per hour, more than Mach 25. This is among the experiences that drive us onward.

We are in our infancy as space travelers. New vehicles will be designed and built to take us into the solar system and eventually beyond. And when they are built there will be pilots eager and up for the challenge of flying them. It won't happen fast enough to satisfy most of us, but it will happen. Humans will reach the stars.

—*George "Pinky" Nelson*, Space Shuttle Astronaut

Sputnik

Model: Sputnik 1
Year: 1957
Registration: None
Serial No.: None

Diameter: 23 inches (35 cm)
Gross Weight: 184 pounds (83.6 kg)
Orbital Speed: 18,000 mph
Antennas: 4 folding rod antennas
two each of 93 inches (2.4 m)
two each of 113 inches (2.9 m)
Location: Museum of Flight
Viewable

Sputnik means "Fellow Traveler"

Few events in modern times have had such a profound effect on history as the monumental breakthrough of October 4, 1957, when the USSR successfully launched the world's first man-made satellite into orbit 560 miles above the earth on a Soviet intercontinental ballistic missile. At that time, the significance of Sputnik I was best described in the French newspaper *Le Figaro*. It reported, "Myth has become reality: Earth's gravity conquered."

Sputnik I orbited over 1,400 times in three months. Launched during the Eisenhower administration when the Cold War was already more than a decade old, Sputnik I did cause a sensation. Yet Sputnik I was planned in 1955 as one of the scientific initiatives during the 1957 International Geophysical Year by the former Soviet Union.

American Response

There was a serious political reaction in America regarding Sputnik. Soon after the launch of Sputnik I, Senator Lyndon B. Johnson warned, "Control of space means control of the world." The United States successfully launched its first satellite, Explorer I on January 31, 1958. Explorer I weighed 30.8 pounds, approximately one-sixth the weight of Sputnik I.

The ability of the Soviets to launch heavier satellites alarmed American space policy officials. In response, President Eisenhower created the National Air and Space Administration. **NASA was born October 1, 1958.**

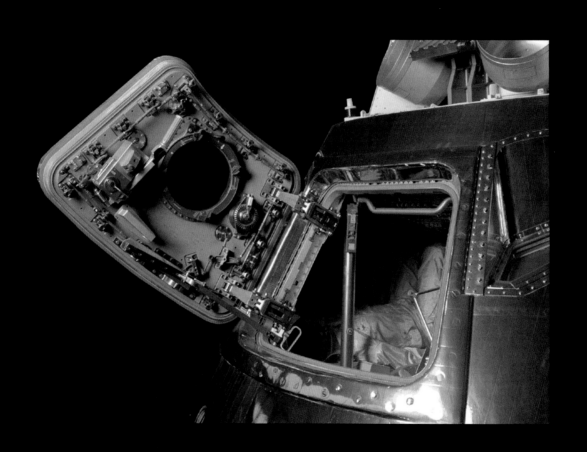

Apollo Command Module

Manufacturer: Rockwell
Model: Apollo Command Module
Year: 1968
Registration: None
Serial No.: 007

Height: 10.58 feet
Diameter: 12.83 feet
Splashdown Weight: 11700 pounds
Gross Weight: 12800 pounds
Location: Museum of Flight
Viewable

A Shape to Beat the Heat

The Apollo Command Module (ACM) shape was created by Maxine Faget, the designer who first developed the blunt-body shape for manned spacecraft during the 1950s. This shape—used in the earlier Mercury and Gemini spacecraft, and even before that in ballistic missile cones—was conceived to meet the demands of extreme temperatures and speeds of space travel. When an ACM reentered Earth's atmosphere, it traveled at nearly 25,000 mph. It was designed with a blunt heat shield base to absorb the shock and the 5,000 degree temperatures generated by the friction of reentry. The command module also had to be maneuverable so it could reenter the atmosphere at a precise angle: too steep and the spacecraft would encounter too much friction and burn up; too shallow and it would bounce off Earth's atmosphere back into space.

A Life of Service

Apollo Command Module 007 was delivered to NASA in 1966. After serving as a ground test vehicle, it was modified in 1967 and delivered to the Gulf of Mexico where it played a key role in training astronauts for splashdown and recovery. Astronauts learned how to climb out of the ACM, signal rescue forces, and survive for several days on the open seas. Such training prepared the astronauts for the possibility of a splashdown far from the planned recovery site.

In 1971, ACM 007 was transported to Eglin Air Force Base in Florida, where it was exposed to cold water and air during testing for the forthcoming Skylab program. The command module survived those extremes only to end up in an equipment lot of the Houston Department of Public Works, where it remained for twelve years. In 1988, Apollo Command Module 007 was restored for the Museum by the Kansas Cosmosphere and Space Center.

Resurs-500

Accession k 1993-10-5b
Manufacturer: Resurs
Model: 500
Year: 1992

Mass: 6300 kilograms
Diameter: 7 feet
Perigee: 177 kilometers
Inclination: 82.6 degrees
Location: Museum of Flight
Viewable

Gifts From Space

In November of 1992, Resurs-500, a Russian spacecraft, orbited the Earth 111 times before splashing down off the coast of Washington State. Inside the round descent vehicle, padded metal boxes contained cultural gifts and messages of greetings from the people of Russia. The day after splashdown, the gifts were presented to the United States in an international ceremony held at the Museum of Flight.

Donated by Nikolai Smirnov of Samara, Russia.

Lady, you want me to answer you if this old airplane is safe to fly?

Just how in the world do you think it got to be this old?

-Anon

Restoration

The Museum's restoration facility at Paine Field in Everett, Washington, is the site where thousands of volunteer hours are devoted to renovating aircraft. Each project is a labor of love, sometimes requiring several years to complete. A group of dedicated volunteers works Tuesday through Saturday to restore each craft to exhibition quality.

Every aircraft that is brought to the 23,000 square foot facility undergoes a thorough evaluation in order to determine the nature of the work needed to be done. A restoration team is assembled and work begins. About fifty volunteers, many of them former Boeing employees, work on between three and five projects at a time.

Past projects have included the Boeing 247D, which required an extensive overhaul that took more than a decade to complete. Current projects include the de Havilland Comet, a Link trainer, and the Chance Vought XF8U-1 Crusader Prototype.

Museum of Flight volunteers are restoring the Boeing B-29 bomber "T-Square-54" in a fenced area just south of the Museum of Flight. Their goal is to restore the aircraft to its original 1945 configuration, with most major systems operable. Although the Museum does not intend to fly the aircraft, the restorations completed by the volunteers are to flight standards.

Expanding. . .

In June 2002, the Museum of Flight broke ground on the first phase of a three-part, $140 million, master expansion plan that will more than double the size of the Museum facility by 2010, making it the largest air and space museum in the world. The first phase of this ambitious expansion is the Personal Courage Wing, an 88,000-square-foot addition at the north end of the Museum's existing campus. Slated to open to the public in the spring of 2004, the Personal Courage Wing will provide a Seattle home for the aircraft of the Museum's Champlin Fighter Collection.

The second phase of the expansion, to be launched after the completion of the Personal Courage Wing, will be the Red Barn Pavilion. This steel-and-glass structure will join the existing Great Gallery and the new Personal Courage Wing, completely enclosing the Red Barn—the 1909 all-wood factory building that is the birthplace of The Boeing Co., and the Museum's largest artifact. The Red Barn Pavilion will not only protect this historical treasure but will also create an additional 22,000 square-feet of gallery space to tell the regional story of aviation in the Pacific Northwest.

The final phase of the Museum's expansion will be a Commercial Aviation Wing, across East Marginal Way, to the northwest of the existing Museum campus. This enormous structure, which will be connected to the Personal Courage Wing via a skybridge, will ultimately house the very large artifacts of the Museum's unparalleled commercial aircraft collection—including the prototypes of the Boeing 727, 737 and 747 airliners—as well as a dedicated Space Gallery.

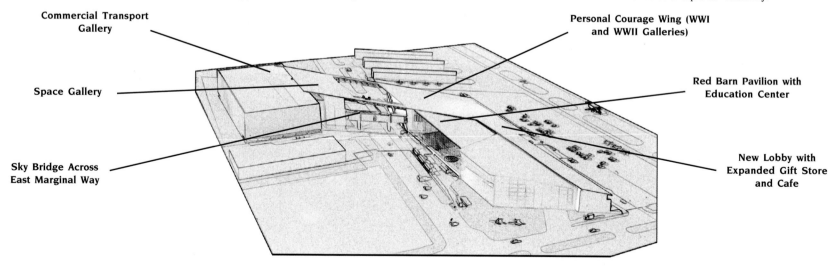

Commercial Transport Gallery

Space Gallery

Sky Bridge Across East Marginal Way

Personal Courage Wing (WWI and WWII Galleries)

Red Barn Pavilion with Education Center

New Lobby with Expanded Gift Store and Cafe

Museum of Flight Expansion

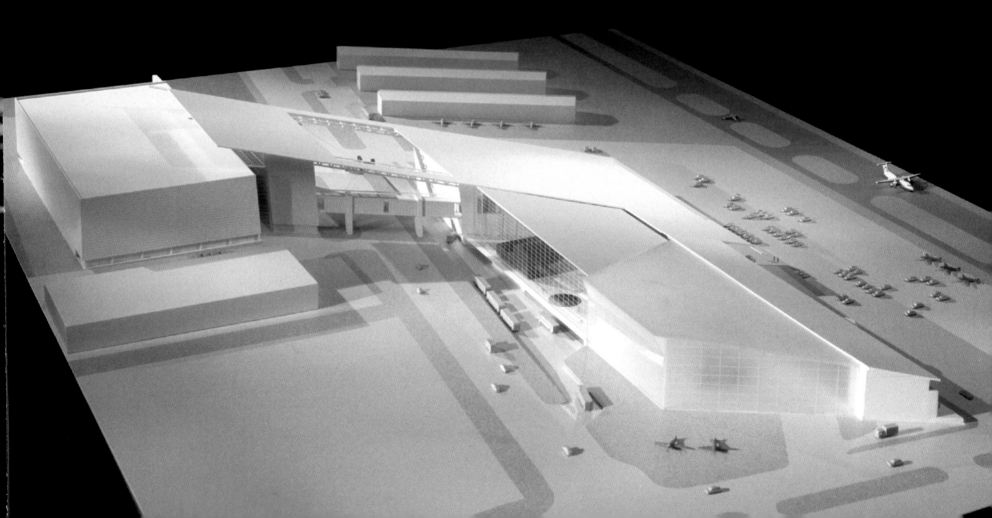

For the love of flying.

Mike Hendrickson and Jeff Huey
Stonebridge